# When All Hope Is Lost

by

George Watson

DORRANCE
PUBLISHING CO
EST. 1920
PITTSBURGH, PENNSYLVANIA 15238

Dorrance Publishing Co
585 Alpha Drive
Pittsburgh, PA 15238
Visit our website at www.dorrancebookstore.com

ISBN: 979-8-88729-292-2
eISBN: 979-8-88729-792-7

# Table of Contents


The Agreement — 3

Paul and Cameron's Home — 7

At The Church Picnic — 11

At the Basketball Court — 25

Paul and Cameron's Home — 17

Night Club — 21

At the Church — 23

Pastor McDaniel's Office — 25

Youth Sunday School Classroom — 29

The Vanishing — 31

Outside in the Parking Lot — 31

Paul and Cameron's Home — 35

At Peter's Home — 41

At the Cemetery — 43

Paul and Cameron's Home — 45

The Reign of the Serpent — 51

At the Christian Rebel Base — 55

Government Base — 59

The Bible Study — 61

The Christians' Secret Meeting — 63

The Antichrist Secret Meeting — 67

The Decision — 69

The Plan — 73

Getting There 77

The Two Witnesses and the Trap 81

The Betrayal 83

The Death of the Witnesses/Inta Tsirhc War on the Saints 89

The Meeting 95

The Forest 99

The Prison 103

Grace Base 107

Betrayal at the Base 113

The Maximum-Security Prison 117

The Gathering 121

The Judgment 125

The New Earth 131

# The Agreement

On a Saturday at eleven-thirty a.m. in a park, three men named Paul White, Peter Moore, and James Woods are playing a game of basketball. Paul, Peter, and James have been best friends since the third grade now, and they all are twenty-seven years old. Paul White is a devout Christian, a successful real estate broker; he is happily married to a lady named Cameron White, and he is the Youth Pastor at New Creation Church where he attends. Peter Moore is not a Christian, but does believe that God exists, but chooses not to serve him. He is a successful tax attorney with a winning record of 99.9 percent of his cases. With that record under his belt, Peter has a huge clientele of people calling for him to be their legal defense attorney. James Woods is not a Christian as well, but he, too, believes in God. James doesn't understand some things about Salvation, and he will not talk to anybody about it. Until he gets an understanding about Salvation, he chooses to remain unsaved. James is a manager at a prestigious bank. James has also invested money in the bank a couple of years ago and other businesses as well, which is the reason why he has accumulated a lot of money. These three young men are at the park on the basketball court playing a game of twenty-one. All of them are tied at twenty. For some reason, none of them was able to make the free-throw shot. Peter now has the ball, and he shoots it from the three-point range; he makes it in, and now he goes from the three-point range to the free-throw line to make the shot.

Peter begins to say, "This is how you swish, swish, swish, and swish; now this game is about to be over!" Peter then shoots the ball; he misses, and James gets the rebound.

James starts talking sarcastically, "Well, well, well, would you look at that, Paul, I got the rebound. I guess the game is not over." James steps back and shoots from the three-point range, and he makes it in, as he walks to the free-throw line casually. James begins to say, "Now that I'm going to the line, this game is officially over," and the other guys say, "Yeah right." James says, "You can say yeah right all you want to, but I'm calling this game over because I know it is over." James shoots the shot from the free-throw line, and he misses!

Paul begins to tell James, sarcastically, "What happened, James? I thought the game was over?" Peter instantly breaks out in laughter at what Paul said to James.

Paul continued to say, "Rebound and I got the ball." Paul then shoots the ball right back up and makes it in. Paul says, "I guess I'm going to the free-throw line," but then Paul shoots the shot, and he misses.

Then James gets the rebound and says, "Time out!" James states, "This is starting to get old, because all three of us have missed the shot at the free-throw line, so I'm proposing an idea."

Peter says, "What kind of idea is it that you are proposing, James?"

"What I am proposing is that we make this game a sudden-death game. Whoever makes the next shot, the game is officially over."

Peter decided to add to the sudden-death game by stating, "Since Paul doesn't bet, let us make an agreement," and everyone says okay. Peter continues to say, "Whoever makes the shot, that person can decide on where we should go tomorrow, and it doesn't matter what that person decides, we all are going." James and Paul both agreed to the deal. James then throws the ball to the backboard, and all three of them begin boxing out to get the rebound. Paul was able to get the ball. When Paul got the rebound, he did his post-game on Peter, so when Paul saw James coming toward him, Paul did a sky hook, and the ball went in the basket, to give Paul the win. Paul then says, "Well, guys, that's game."

James sarcastically begins to say, "Yeah, yeah. All you did was throw up that prayer shot."

Peter said, "Yeah, that little prayer shot, we all know that you are no Magic Johnson or Kareem," as Peter and James laugh repeatedly.

Paul begins to laugh sarcastically and states, "I may not be a Magic Johnson or a Kareem, but I know what I am, though, the winner of this basketball game, which you both are not." All three men start wiping the sweat from their faces, drinking their Gatorades, and they all begin walking back to the car.

Paul begins to say, "Now seeing that I won the game, I think this is a good time to discuss the place where we are going tomorrow. On tomorrow, gentleman, I will be seeing both of you at my church, New Creation, and church time is at eleven-fifteen a.m. sharp. Now don't be afraid to wear a suit and a tie, and please don't be late, because I will be looking for the both of you."

James begins to ask Paul, "Are there any other place besides church that we can go?"

Peter says, "Yeah, like going to a movie, a restaurant, a library, or a museum. Paul, we will go anywhere, but don't drag us to church, man."

Then Paul says to the guys, "Think about it, I'm not dragging you to church because I'm not the one who made the sudden-death game agreement in the first place. You did, Peter."

James says, "I didn't do it, so why do I have to go to church?"

Paul began to explain to James, "You agreed to it, and that is why we are all going to church."

James begins to look at Peter, shaking his head. Paul then gets in his car, turns on the ignition, and rolls down the window, further stating to James and Peter, "Since we all agreed to it, it doesn't matter who initiated it." Then he looked at his watch and realized that he was late for his church's annual picnic, and so he ends their meeting by saying, "Again, I will see the both of you tomorrow morning with a suit and tie on at my church at eleven-fifteen a.m. Bye." Paul then drives off to go home and change.

# Paul and Cameron's Home

Paul's home is a one-story home that is white with three bedrooms and two and a half bathrooms in it. Paul unlocks the front door and sees his wife Cameron asleep on the couch. Paul goes over to the couch where she is sleeping and gently, ever so gently, kisses her on the forehead. Cameron awakes and kisses him on the lips and says, "Hey, sweetie. How was the game with the guys today?"

"It was fun and interesting," which then peeked Cameron's interest, and she asks, "Oh, really? How so?"

Paul then begins to break down what happened. "It was a tie game. Each of us had twenty points apiece, and for some reason nobody couldn't make the free-throw shot. The game was going so long, and we all had other important things that we each needed to do today. So, James suggested we make the game 'sudden death,' where whoever makes the next shot wins the game. Peter then added a stipulation to the game. He said whoever wins the game, the winner is allowed to choose a place for all of us to go together tomorrow, no matter where it is, what it is, or the time. Everybody else would have to go."

Cameron went on to say, "You know that stipulation was meant for you," as she begins walking into the kitchen to get some water. She says, "Peter and James will go to a nightclub in a minute, and it was also a trap to bring you along with them."

Paul then says, "I figured that one out when Peter made that stipulation, but I agreed to it anyways. But see, Peter and James forgot about the hook shot my grandfather taught me when I was a boy."

Cameron then chimes in and says, "I'm going to take a guess and say that you won the game. Let me also guess that the place that they are going tomorrow is church? Now, are my guesses correct?"

"Yes, yes, yes," Paul says. "Your guesses are correct. I won, and yes, they are going to church tomorrow. I knew that I was going to win because that hook shot that my grandfather taught me always goes in. Now I will see them tomorrow at eleven-fifteen for church."

As Paul is heading to the bathroom to get washed up for his church annual picnic, Cameron follows him because she feels that they are being forced to go to church, so she wants to discuss this issue with him. So, Cameron begins to state, "Really, Paul, this is how you get your friends to come to church, through trickery? I would never have thought that you would stoop that low to get them to come to church."

Paul turns around, looks at Cameron, and says, "Okay, let us get one thing straight. I did not do any trickery on anybody. Peter gave the stipulation to the game, me and James agreed to it, and that is all. I know how my best friends play basketball, and that is because I have played with them for years. Which means that I know how they move on the court. They also know about my grandfather's hook shot and that he taught it to me. They just forgot that I remembered it is all. Since I won the game, the stipulation allowed me to choose the place and time where we are going to meet tomorrow. I chose church because I want them to hear about Jesus."

Cameron then says, "They couldn't hear it from you Paul?"

Paul then says to Cameron, "Yes, you're right, they could, and they already have. I wanted them to hear it from my Pastor now, and you already know that they will not come to church, let alone to the church picnic today. When Peter came up with that stipulation, I figured that this was a good opportunity for me to get them to come to church. It was like God made a way for me to get them to come to church and hear from my Pastor. The Bible says that we should be wise as serpents but gentle as a dove. What I displayed today was wisdom that was given by God."

After that conversation, Cameron then scoffs. "Always using the Bible to back you up on everything."

Paul then says, "You know it, Cameron, and what is wrong with that?"

Cameron says, "Nothing is wrong with it, but do you have to use it to solve everything in your life?"

Paul continues, "Yes, I do, Cameron. It is the truth that I live by; it is my road map to God. It is my basic instruction before leaving the earth, and the more I read the more I know who God is."

Cameron states, "I know that." Then she noticed some clothes were laid out on the bed, and she asks Paul "What are you doing today?"

"Oh, I'm going to the church's annual picnic. I forgot that you don't go to church anymore. I have a question for you, baby. Do you even pray or read your Bible anymore?"

Cameron then sits on the bed and tells Paul, "Don't start with me."

Now Paul and Cameron go back and forth.

"Start what with you? I'm not starting anything with you. I just asked a question, Cameron. Now I want to make a statement of what I see, Cameron. You don't go to church anymore for some reason. You don't even pray anymore, nor do you read your Bible. I can say that because you used to have a set time, which was at five in the morning and nine at night, when you would would be reading your Bible, which always came behind the prayer. Now you don't do either one. So, I want to know what happened." Paul then turns around to go into the bathroom and then turns back around to Cameron and says, 'You know, it was you who inspired me to read and pray more. Remember before we started dating, you told me we couldn't get married because we were unequally yoked? That next Sunday, I came to church and got saved. I started having a prayer and word life. God used you to get me to come to Him, and it worked. Now you lost it. So, again, I ask you, what is going on?"

Cameron replies with, "First, let me say that I am very proud and happy of the fact that God has brought you this far in life, because we both know where you would end up if God never showed up in your life. Now, as for me, my mom forced me to go to church at the age of fourteen. I got saved, and I did say that to you, Paul. I have seen things that have made me question my faith. I also have learned that there is more to life than just being saved and going to church."

Paul looks at her, and with sadness in his voice says, "Cameron, you sound like the old me, not the woman that I met thirteen years ago, and you are not the woman whom I married four years ago."

Then Cameron looks at Paul and asks him, "What are you saying, Paul?"

And Paul continues, saying, "What I am saying is that I can't be, and I won't be"—as he holds back tears—"unequally yoked."

Paul then turns around and goes to the bathroom to get ready for his church picnic. As he is heading toward the bathroom, both are sad after Paul tearfully said what he had to say. When Paul came out of the bathroom from washing up, Cameron is sitting on the bed, waiting for him. As she continues to speak, "Paul, I understand what you are saying, so let us do this. Tomorrow"—as Cameron goes over to Paul and grabs his hands—"I want to go to church with you tomorrow, and we will go from there. Is that okay?"

Paul looks at her and says, "Okay." Cameron, we will go tomorrow, and I love you."

"I love you too, Paul," says Cameron.

# At The Church Picnic

At the park, New Creation Church is having their annual church picnic. Some of the men in the church are setting up the tables for the food, and some of the women are at the food tables getting the food ready. The rest of the people are either walking around the park or lying on their blankets under a shady tree. As Paul drives up to the park, Pastor Jonathan McDaniel is standing on the sidewalk, watching Paul park his car. After parking the car, Paul gets out the car as Pastor McDaniel greets Paul with a smile on his face. The Pastor speaks to Paul, saying, "Hello, Elder White," and Paul says hello back. The Pastor continues to say, "How is everything going with you?"

Paul says, "I am blessed, Pastor. No complaints with me, Pastor."

As Pastor McDaniel continues to talk to Paul, he says, "That is good to hear, Elder. Paul, walk with me back to the picnic area. I need to talk to you about something."

Paul says, "Is everything okay?" as they both turn and walk towards the church picnic area.

Pastor McDaniel continues to speak with Paul. "I'm fine, Paul, no need to worry, but I want to talk to you about some changes that I am doing in the church. One of those changes concerns you."

Paul points to himself, asking, "Did I do something wrong?"

The Pastor chuckles. "Paul, you did nothing wrong. I just wanted to talk to you about being the church's new Assistant Pastor. Is that okay with you?"

Then they both stop walking, and Paul begins to speak his mind, stating, "I don't know, Pastor. It is just that you have never had an assistant before. I have just two questions for you, why now, and why me?"

Pastor McDaniel's response to him was "I know that I've never had an assistant before, but I must pass the baton to someone. God has chosen you to be that leader that this community needs. Last night at home, I was on my knees, asking the Lord to show me who is going to be the Assistant Pastor of the church. A minute after I prayed that prayer, you dropped into my spirit like lightning. I had the bedroom door closed, and when I opened it, the First Lady was standing right there. She told me that God spoke to her while she was in the kitchen and said to her, 'Paul White, the Assistant Pastor.' When she told me what the Lord said to her, I told her that I was just praying to God about choosing the Assistant Pastor. I realized that it was a definite confirmation that God has chosen you to be the Assistant Pastor."

Paul became excited and said with a smile on his face, "This is a huge honor for me, Pastor, and the fact that God has chosen me to be the new Assistant Pastor of New Creation Church. I accept it, Pastor. I have one question for you, who is going to take my place as the Youth Pastor?"

Pastor McDaniel then says, "That is the same question I asked the Lord last night, and then the Lord dropped Elder Dixon in my spirit. Elder Dixon is the one who is going to take your place as the new Youth Pastor of the church. Paul, can you tell Elder Dixon about the change? And I will announce this to the church tomorrow."

Paul says, "Okay," and they both continue walking toward the church picnic area. When they reach the picnic area, First Lady McDaniel greets Paul, hugs him, and kisses him on the cheek.

Pastor McDaniel says, "Well, I see there is no kiss for me. I guess I'll just mosey on to the dessert table and get a little sample taste of Mother Morrow's peach cobbler."

Pastor walks off on his way to the dessert table, but not before the First Lady lays down the law and states, "Pastor, you better stay out of Mother Morrow's cobbler, or you will not receive another kiss from this First Lady."

Then the First Lady looks back at Paul and continues their conversation, as Paul states, "I am blessed, and with all this food I see, I'll be extremely blessed before the day is over," as Paul is smiling, looking at the food.

First Lady McDaniel is looking for Paul's wife, Cameron. Then First Lady says to Paul, "I see that you cannot wait to eat. I know that your wife has more self-control than you. By the way, where is she? Where is Cameron?"

Paul states to the First Lady that Cameron couldn't make it to the picnic. "But you will see her at church tomorrow."

"Okay, says the First Lady, "but when you get home today, let her know that I need to speak to her before church starts."

Paul tells The First Lady, "Okay, that will be the first thing I do when I get home. Now, before I eat," says Paul, "I need to speak to William. Do you know where he is?"

The First Lady says, "Yes, I do. He is at the basketball court with the young people." Paul then says thank you, and he walks off toward the basketball court.

# At the Basketball Court

As Paul is walking toward the basketball court, he noticed Elder Dixon is on the grass teaching some young people the story of Samson. While Elder Dixon is teaching some of the young people, there are also some young people on the basketball court playing ball. As the young people are playing, Paul notices one of the young women shoot a ball from three-point range over a man who was guarding her. Paul laughs and says, "I saw that, Jeff. Ashley shot that three-point right in your face."

Jeff then says sarcastically, "Yeah, yeah, yeah. That was just a lucky shot. Now that I got the ball, watch me take it to the hole on her." Paul is now standing there, watching the young girl Ashley defend against Jeff. Jeff goes to the basket to make the layup, but Ashley steals the ball from him before he can do it.

Then Ashley innocently says, "How are you going to take me to the hole without the ball, Jeff?" Ashley further digs in and says, "Since I got the ball back, I'm just going to shoot another three-point shot." Ashley takes a step back and shoots the ball, all the while Jeff is guarding her. Ashley shoots the ball, and the ball goes in.

Paul is laughing and says, "Well, it looks like Ashley got you again, Jeff. Now what are you going to say this time, luck or skill?" Paul is laughing his head off at Jeff.

Jeff then looks across the way and sees church members at the food table in line to eat. Then Jeff states, "What I'm going to say is… I want a rematch, but first, I want something to eat, because I'm hungry."

And Ashley rubs her stomach too and says to Jeff, "Okay, Jeff, eat first, then rematch later, because I'm hungry, too." Then all the young people agree and go to the food table to get a plate. Before Elder Dixon goes to get something to eat, Paul goes over to talk to him.

"Hello, William, let me talk to you before we go eat."

"Sure, Paul," William says.

"Listen, the Pastor was talking to me a few minutes ago. He elevated me to the position of being the new Assistant Pastor of the church."

William happily replied, "That's wonderful! I am happy for you, Paul, but I have a question. If you are going to be the new Assistant Pastor of the church, who is going to take your place as the Youth Pastor?"

Paul shares with William the rest of his conversation he had with Pastor. "I said the exact same thing to the Pastor, and he suggested that the man who should take my place as the Youth Pastor is you, William."

William then points to himself, looking shocked.

"Yes, you, William. Not only did the Pastor suggest you, but I also suggested you, too. I feel, I know that you will make a good Youth Pastor."

William began feeling unsure and tells Paul, "I don't know about that, Paul. I don't know if I am the right man for the job. I mean, are you sure about suggesting me?"

Paul's answer to William is an emphatical, "Yes, I'm sure about suggesting you take my place. I mean you know the Word of God, you love young people, and you are a man of wisdom, except when you rooted for the Golden State Warriors to win the NBA Championship," as they both started laughing.

William begins to say, "Here we go with this again. You just won't let it go, will you?"

Then Paul answers, "You got that right, Will, and I am not going to let it go too soon."

Then William says to Paul, "Well, if you and Pastor both suggested it, then I believe that it is a God-ordained move. To put it in short, I accept."

Paul then pats William on the back and says, "Now we go get something to eat because I can sure smell the food all the way from here. Just like Jeff, I'm hungry, and I know you are, too, so let's go eat," as they both went to go eat at the food tables.

# Paul and Cameron's Home

Paul comes home and goes right into the bathroom. After Paul takes his shower, he goes into the living room to watch some TV. Paul's wife Cameron is in the kitchen, fixing her dinner. Cameron talks to her husband Paul and says, "Hey, Paul. You went right into the shower, so you can't even tell your wife hello and give her a kiss?"

Paul begins to chuckle as he goes over to his wife and kisses her. "I apologize for that, Cameron, but I was so sweaty and stinky after the church's picnic. Me, William, and the young people played five back-to-back full-court basketball games after we finished eating. Some of the young people didn't feel like playing, so they sat on the grass and watched the games. William's team were the ones that were having Bible study with him earlier versus my team who didn't want to have Bible study. All they wanted to do was play basketball."

Cameron chimes in and says, "Okay, good thing you did take that shower because I don't need this house smelling like wet dogs," as Paul began to laugh sarcastically.

Paul then says to Cameron, "You know, you can stay in the kitchen because I don't want the living smelling like hot garlic."

After Paul made that statement, Cameron feels the need to go over to Paul in the living room to give him a hug, and she says, "You know you like garlic anyways, so stop fronting like you don't."

Paul gets over the garlic issue and tells Cameron that he has something important to share with her. He begins to tell her, "The Pastor told me today that he has chosen me to be the Assistant Pastor of the church, and I accepted the assignment."

Cameron then seems a bit petard, as she slightly pushes away from Paul. Cameron is set aback and stated to Paul, "Assistant Pastor, huh, and you accepted the position without even talking to me?"

Paul then says to his wife, "Yes, Cameron, I did take the position without talking to you first, but I was so excited when the Pastor told me about how miraculous the confirmation came about. I knew it was God in him choosing me to be the Assistant Pastor, so much so, that I accepted it without discussing it with you, and for that I apologize. Cameron, I honestly didn't think that it mattered."

Cameron then gets very upset and states to Paul, "Of course it mattered, Paul. It mattered because I feel like you only took the position without consulting me, all because you want me to come to church again. Paul, I feel that you saw this as an opportunity to get me to come back in church and I think that is very wrong and deceitful."

Paul then expresses to his wife, "Listen, Cameron, when I took this position, I did not have you in mind. All I thought about was doing the will of God, that's all. This is in no way a ploy or opportunity to get you to come to church. I believe this is God's will for me; besides, this was confirmed through the Pastor and the First Lady on the same night. You must understand this, Cameron, I want to stay in God's will, and nothing else is more important than that." After that, Paul goes and sits on the couch to watch TV.

The conversation prompts Cameron, and she goes and sits next to Paul on the couch, and then she grabs the remote to turn off the TV to say something further to Paul on the subject. "Paul, I thought that the only reason you accepted the position to be the Assistant Pastor was to get me to start going back to church. I understand that it was God's will for you to become Assistant Pastor, and you just want to stay in His Will. I don't want to stand in your way of that, so I apologize for accusing you and getting mad at you."

As they hug, Cameron asks Paul to forgive her and Paul says, "I forgive you, Cameron," but before Paul turns on the TV, he has something else that he wants to tell Cameron.

"Oh yeah, I forgot to tell you that First Lady McDaniel was looking for you at the picnic."

Cameron then has a surprised look on her face, as she states, "The First Lady? Why was she looking for me?"

Paul tells Cameron, "I don't know why she said that, but she said that since you weren't at the picnic today, she told me to give you the message that she wants to talk to you before service starts tomorrow in her office." Paul then sits down to watch TV, and Cameron is in the kitchen, wondering what the First Lady wants to talk to her about.

# Night Club

Later that night, across town at a nightclub called The Forbidden Fruit, inside the club the lights were dim, the music was loud, people are on the floor dancing, and some of them had a cup of an alcoholic beverage in their hand. In the middle of the dance floor surrounded by beautiful women we see James's dancing, while Peter is sitting in a booth, in a dark corner. James approaches Peter, very excited, shocked, and amused at the same time. James says, "Wow, this is a twist and an interesting site to see."

Peter then says, "Not tonight, James," as James begins to look irritated. "I don't have time for this," and then James sits down in the booth and begins to laugh a little.

"I'm sorry, Peter. It is just that you are always the one on the dance floor surrounded by beautiful women, not me. When I saw this, I just had to say something, but seriously, is everything okay?"

Then Peter looks at James and says, "I know that I'm not myself tonight, because my mind is on something else. Five years ago, I promised myself that I would never step foot into a church again. Now five years later, and what am I doing, stepping foot into a church. This is something that I promised myself I would never do."

James tells him, "Well, Peter, if you feel this way, then why did you add that stipulation to the agreement? We both knew that if Paul won, he was going to choose church."

Peter answers, "I made that stipulation to the agreement because I figured that one of us was going to win. I did not think that Paul would win. I thought that if one of us"—as Peter pointed to himself and James—"had won we would have chosen either a strip club or a nightclub; that's why I added that stipulation. I did not think about Paul at all, and his annoying hook shot. I would think by now you and Paul both know how I feel about Christianity, let alone go to a church service. Why would Paul choose church out of all places?"

Then James says to Peter, "I understand where you're coming from, Peter, but the funny thing about this is the fact that Paul will never stop finding ways to get us to go to church. Remember how he tried to use his birthday to get us to go to church with him, but we made that stipulation that he can make any wish and we will honor it except go to church? You made that stipulation before he could say it, and by the way, it was a good save," as Peter and James start laughing about the story.

Peter says, raising his cup, "Well, that's Paul for you; he never stops nor gives up." As they both agree, they both drink to that fact. Peter then gets up from the table and says, "Well, we better head home, because we got church in the morning at eleven-thirty." James stands up, and they both leave the club.

# At the Church

Now the members are coming into the sanctuary at New Creation Baptist Church, and people are pulling up into the parking lot to go to church. Paul, along with Cameron, pulls up into the church parking lot for Sunday school. Pastor McDaniel, extending himself outside right next to the church door, greets people as they come inside the church. Paul and Cameron get out of their car, then they approach Pastor McDaniel and greet him before going into the church, and Paul says to Pastor, "Hello Pastor, I see you're not tired from the picnic yesterday."

Then Pastor McDaniel states back, "Hello, Elder White. I should be saying the same thing to you, playing five basketball games back-to-back.... Well, well, well, I see you there, Sister White, and how are you doing today?"

Cameron answers Pastor McDaniel, saying, "Hello, Pastor. I am doing well. Thank you for asking."

Pastor McDaniel continues, "Man, it has been a long time since you've been here at the church. How long has it been, Elder White, since the last time we've seen at the church?"

Paul then looks at Cameron and says, "I don't know, Pastor. Maybe about... ten or eleven months."

Pastor McDaniel then says to Cameron, "Well, it doesn't matter how long it's been, I'm just glad to see you, and I know that the First Lady feels the same way. Matter of fact, she's waiting on you right now in my office."

Cameron then tells Pastor, "Okay, I am heading there right now, Pastor. I will talk to you after service."

Paul then continues his conversation with Pastor, saying, "I know that Elder Dixon is teaching the youth class because it is his week. I think I will mosey on down there to make sure that he is ready for his new office as the new Youth Pastor."

Pastor McDaniel then responds to Paul, saying, "Okay, Elder White, you do that, but are you ready for your new office as well?"

Paul responds and says to Pastor, "I'm going to be honest with you, I was a little nervous, but I know that I can do it."

"Of course you can," says Pastor McDaniel to Paul. "You can do it; with God on your side, it will be done. Now you go and make sure that Elder Dixon is ready."

When Paul walks away, Pastor McDaniel goes back to greeting people who are coming in for service.

# Pastor McDaniel's Office

Inside Pastor McDaniel's office, First Lady McDaniel is sitting on the couch, reading her Bible. Cameron knocks on the door, and The First Lady says, "It's open. Come on in."

Cameron comes in, and she notices that a lot has changed inside the office. There are pictures of the Pastor with his wife on a cruise, a picture of the Pastor and his wife with their children and grandchildren at an amusement park, and a bookcase filled with books. Those books are Bibles, encyclopedias, dictionaries, commentaries, and other books from different authors inside of the bookcase. Cameron breaks her silence and says, "Hello, First Lady. I was told that you wanted to see me before service."

First Lady says, "Yes, I did, Cameron. Please take a seat." As Cameron sits down on the couch, she goes on to ask her, "Tell me, how is everything going with you?"

Cameron pleasantly replies, "Everything's going fine. I have no complaints."

Then the First Lady asks her a question, stating, "Did Paul tell you that he has been asked to be the new Assistant Pastor of the church?"

Cameron says, "Yes, he told me, and at first, I thought that it was a ploy to get me to come back to church. But then Paul told me that it wasn't, it was just the will of God, that's all."

The First Lady then assures her, "Yes, it is the will of God for Paul to become Assistant Pastor of the church. That is not the reason why I wanted to talk to you. The conversation that we are about to have right now is about you."

As Cameron is curious about what First Lady has said to her, she is still in shock, as she replies, "About me? What about me?"

The First Lady continues, "Cameron, we both know that you have backslid in this past year." Cameron then has a shocked look on her face, as First Lady continues, "About two weeks ago, God have been giving me dreams about you. Cameron, I have been having dreams of you going to clubs, drinking, smoking, and using foul language. This past week alone, I dreamed that you had gotten so drunk at a party that you almost cheated on your husband."

Cameron cannot believe the First Lady said what she said, and Cameron tries to keep her face straight, but she had a shocked look of guilt on her face. The First Lady went on to say, "That was why you spent the night at your friend Andrea's house, because you didn't want Paul to see you like that."

Now the tears begin to run down Cameron's face when First Lady mentions her husband to her. The First Lady continues to talk to Cameron, saying, "Cameron, I am not here to judge you, or make you feel bad. I just want to talk to you. Cameron, I have known you since you were twelve years old, and at fifteen is when you gave your life to the Lord. Since then, you have always had a fire for God, Cameron. I have seen God use you to cast out devils, lay hands on the sick, and even prophesy to people. I just want to know what happened. What made you lose your zeal for God? What caused you to fall back? Because I believe something tragic must have happened to you that even your husband doesn't know. Remember this, what is said in this room stays in this room."

Before Cameron can say anything, she first wipes the tears from her eyes, and then she commences to say, "Well, First Lady, you would think it started when my mother passed away, but that's not the case. When my mother died, I was inspired by my mom even more when I heard all the stories about her zeal and love for God. What happened was I had seen so many people who had been used by God fall by the wayside or being used by God, but behind closed doors, they acted a totally different way, and I got discouraged. It discouraged me so bad to the point where I began to question myself, am I pleasing God, or am I doing this to please my mother? My reply to myself was this: I'm just going to step back and think about it. I guess that's when I stepped back. I kept stepping further, further, and further away until I stepped away from God completely. I couldn't tell Paul because it was my devotion to God that inspired Paul to be saved in the first place, so I didn't want to discourage him. I had decided to keep it all to myself."

The First Lady began to minister to Cameron, saying, "Well, first off, I think you didn't take the time to grieve the loss of your mother."

Then Cameron begins to cry, and the First Lady embraces her. She embraces her like a mother embraces her child when the child is hurt. Secondly, the First lady said Cameron, "You cannot look at other people and what they are doing because all that is going to do is burden you down. Cameron, you cannot be burdened down by the sins of others. You are supposed to keep your eyes fixed on God, and the moment you start looking at other people and not on God, you will fall. Those are the enemy's tactics to discourage you and snatch your place out of the Kingdom of God. The reason I've been having these dreams is because God says it is time for you to come back to him. Cameron, it is time for you to come back to God before time is up, and we don't know when Jesus it's going to come back. I know people have been saying that for years, but if you look at the news, the news will tell you that it's getting closer and closer, and that Jesus is about to return."

"Cameron, again, I tell you to get it together and get it right before time is up."

Both ladies begin to embrace each other one more time. "I am only telling you this because I love you, Cameron, and you have always been like a daughter to me."

Cameron then reciprocates her feelings to the First Lady, telling her, "I love you too, First Lady, and you have been like a mom to me. About what you said, let me think about it first, and I'll see you in church."

"All right, Cameron, but don't think too long because you don't know when your time is up," as Cameron leaves the office to go inside the sanctuary.

# Youth Sunday School Classroom

In the youth Sunday school class, William is wrapping the class up with final thoughts. Paul comes in as the class was letting out. William looked at Paul and continues, "I know that some of you must go to the restroom, but please don't take long. Remember, we are reviewing today. I need everyone inside the sanctuary when all the Sunday school classes come together for assembly."

In walks Paul and he goes directly up to William and says, "Hello, Elder White," and Paul says, "Hello, Elder Dixon," as they shake hands and embrace each other.

"I wanted to hear some of the lesson, and tell your young people congratulations on winning the basketball game yesterday at the picnic. The young people on my team want a rematch. It sounds like a good idea, and after the game, we all are going out for lunch. My treat."

William interjects, "That sounds like a challenge, and I know that they will gladly accept it. One thing, though, if my team loses, then I pay for lunch; but if your team loses, you pay for lunch. Does that sound fair, Paul?"

"It is fair either way, William. But I want to ask you, are you ready to be elevated to your new office today as the new Youth Pastor?"

"I don't know, Paul. I am a little nervous about this elevation."

Paul then tells him, "That's good that you're nervous because it shows that all you want is for God to have his way in this department. You know that if you need any help, I got your back."

"Thank you, Paul, for your support. Now I have a question for you. Are you ready to be elevated today to your new office as the Assistant Pastor of the church?"

Paul tells William, "I'm nervous. To tell you the truth, I am a whole lot nervous because the Pastor has never had an Assistant Pastor before. For me to be elevated to this position, it's nerve-racking. Nevertheless, just like God will help you, he also will help me. William says that since this is God's will, I know that we will be fine. Question, when is Pastor going to announce these changes? Pastor told me that he's going to announce it to the church right after this group that he invited finishes their song."

"Who is this group that the Pastor invited, Paul? I mean, did he give you a hint of who the group is?"

Paul responds, "I have no clue. All I know is that he has known them since he was a child, that's all I know."

"Well, we better get inside the sanctuary for the Sunday school assembly, because you have a review to do. I'm just glad it's not me but you who is doing it," and they both laugh and leave out the room.

# The Vanishing

Inside of the sanctuary, all the elders are sitting in the same section, the ministers are sitting in their section, and the choir it's sitting in the choir stand. The First Lady is sitting next to the Pastor. After the recognition of visitors, the Pastor now gets up and heads to the podium to introduce the guest group who are going to minister in song. Pastor McDaniel says to the congregation, "Good morning, everyone, and praise the Lord!" All the audience then responds by saying praise the Lord. Peter and James come in and sit down next to Cameron who is on the far-right middle row. The Pastor continues to say, "I want to thank all of you for coming, especially Paul's two best friends whom he has known since elementary school." Then Pastor McDaniel points to Peter and James. Everyone looks and claps their hands while they both stand up. Both men are smiling and waving their hands as a sign of saying hello to everyone. Pastor continues and states, "I have two important announcements to make before the sacrificial offering, but before I do that, I want to introduce to you a gospel trio. I have known these three women since I was a little boy. God has used them mightily in the past, and he is still using them now. I want to introduce to you 'Perfect Will,' so clap your hands as they come forth to minister to us in song."

Three women walked on stage to sing their song Entitled "Wrong Motives". After Perfect Will finishes singing, Pastor McDaniel goes back to the podium, and the three ladies go to their seats. Pastor McDaniel begins speaking again to the congregation. "Thank you, Perfect Will, for that selection. Everybody, we need to check our motives, because everything must line up with the Word of God, so you better check it before time runs out for you. God has laid it on my heart to have an Assistant Pastor here at this church. The new Assistant Pastor here at New Creation Baptist Church is none other than Elder White." With that announcement, everyone begins clapping their hands for the announcement. "And his replacement for Youth Pastor will be none other than our own Elder Dixon." Everyone is in shock, as they are all standing up and clapping their hands. "I know that this is different, because I have never had an Assistant Pastor here at New Creation, but God has placed it on my heart." Then Pastor McDaniel turns to Elder White and Elder Dixon and instructs Elder White and Elder Dixon to come forward, so he could pray for both men so that God can use them in His own way in their new positions.

Paul and William go up there to get prayed for. As the Pastor is praying for them, the Pastor, First Lady, Paul, William, and half of the church members look up at the same time, hearing a sound. Paul than looks at Cameron, Peter, and James with his eyes bucked wide open. Then Paul, the Pastor, First Lady, William, and half of the church vanish in front of everyone's eyes. The remainder of the congregation that was left begin crying and screaming, for they all knew what had just happened. Cameron turns and looks at Peter and James with tears in her eyes.

After Cameron wipes the tears from her eyes, she comes to reality and says to Peter and James, "Okay, we need to remain calm."

Peter says, "Easier said than done, Cameron. I mean everyone in here has seen their loved ones vanish right before their very eyes."

Cameron replies, "I know they did, Peter, which is why they all need to know what is going to happen next."

James chimes in sarcastically and says, "Oh yeah, and you know, Cameron?"

Then Cameron says, "No, James, I don't, but I know someone who does, and I need everyone's attention. Can you all help me do that?"

Peter and James look at each other, then they look at Cameron, and both nod their heads, signifying that they agree and will help. All three of them go to the podium, and Peter speaks in the microphone to get everyone's attention. He starts by saying, "Excuse me, everyone, but may I have your attention."

One by one, the people stop yelling and crying, and Peter continues to say that Cameron has something to say, as Peter gives her the microphone. Cameron tells the remaining congregation in the sanctuary, "Everyone, we have all seen a loved one vanish before our very eyes, and some of us are even saying,

'God, why did you leave me?' Well to everyone who wants answers on what is going on and what is going to happen next, I invite everyone to come to my house immediately. I promise you all your questions will be answered."

When everyone comes outside, some of the church congregation goes directly to Cameron's house. En route, they see chaos all over in the streets. There were cars colliding with other cars, with buildings and with people. Inside the cars, there is a driver, a passenger, or both missing from the car. All that is there are a pile of clothes on the seat and people injured from the collision. There are people running around, husbands looking for their wives and wives looking for their husbands. Fathers and mothers are looking for their children, and there are teenage children looking for their parents.

In the parking lot of the church, there are people scrambling to get into their cars, but there are also people who don't have cars to get into.

Cameron stands on the top of the trunk of her car, facing everybody, and says loudly, "Okay, for those who have cars, if you have space available in your car, please let the people who do not have a car ride in with you so that they will have a way to my house." Then the people began to make sure every person had a ride. People are getting out of their cars asking others if they had rides to get to Cameron's house. Cameron then begins to thank the people with cars for their cooperation in making sure no one was left behind en route to her house. Everyone finally leaves the church and goes to Cameron's house.

# Paul and Cameron's Home

Cameron unlocks the front door, and then Cameron, Peter, and James direct everyone into the living room, where they are able to watch the television. Once everyone is in the living room, Cameron then turns around to Peter and James, telling them, "Okay, I'm going to need both of you to help me dig this box up that is buried in the backyard." Then Cameron goes to the living room to tell the people that she will be right back, and that she must get something from the backyard, which will only take ten minutes. Cameron, Peter, and James go out of the side door to the backyard. Four shovels are in the backyard leaning on the wall, so they get the shovels, and they start to dig up the box. They are digging right in front of the rose bush. They find a blue toolbox buried in the backyard that is locked.

Peter says to Cameron, "What is locked in this blue toolbox that you have buried in the backyard?"

James chimes in and says, "Yeah, you got us back here digging up an old locked toolbox."

Then Cameron pulls out a key and opens the toolbox. Inside are ten Bibles and a DVD that is in a red case. "This is what was inside the toolbox. Paul and I made this DVD the day after we moved into this house. Now, come on. Let's bring it inside the house so everybody can watch it, and you two"—as she is points at them—"you need to see it as well."

Cameron brings the toolbox into the house where everyone is seated and tells the crowd, "Okay, since it is thirty of you all, I need everyone to get into ten groups of threes." Once they complied with her request, Cameron passes out the Bibles, pens, and scratch paper to each group of people. After that, Cameron turns on the TV and puts in the DVD, and then tells the people,

"When any scripture reference is mentioned, I want you to write it on paper, and when the video is over, we are going to go over them."

Now on the screen appears first her husband, Paul, sitting in a chair inside of an office, wearing a gray shirt and blue jeans, and he begins to speak. "Hello, everyone. If you're watching this video, then that means me and including half of the people on this Earth have vanished. I know that you are upset and sad, saying, 'Where is my loved one?' But I want to tell you that they are fine because we are in the presence of the Lord. In 1 Thessalonians 4:16–18, it states: *For the Lord himself shall descend from heaven with a shout, with the voice of the archangel, and with the trump of God: and the dead in Christ shall rise first: Then we which are alive and remain shall be caught up together with them in the clouds, to meet the Lord in the air: and so, shall we ever be with the Lord. Wherefore comfort one another with these words.*

"This moment in history is known to us as the Rapture of the Saints. Now, you are probably wondering what about the rest of us that are still here on Earth. Therefore, me and my wife Cameron made this DVD for you because we want you to know what's going to happen after the Rapture. After the Rapture, there will be mass hysteria because a lot of people's loved ones have vanished without a trace! In all this hysteria, a man will rise to power. Read 2 Thessalonians 2:6–10, which states: *And now ye know what withholdeth that he might be revealed in his time. For the mystery of iniquity doth already work: only he who now letteth will let, until he be taken out of the way. And then shall that Wicked be revealed, whom the Lord shall consume with the spirit of his mouth and shall destroy with the brightness of his coming: Even him, whose coming is after the working of Satan with all power and signs and lying wonders, and with all deceivableness of unrighteousness in them that perish; because they received not the love of the truth, that they might be saved.* He will be a superb politician; he will amaze the world with his miracles and speeches. People will follow him thinking he is the Messiah, but he's not, he is a master deceiver. He is what the Bible refers to as the antichrist: 1 John 2:18, stating: *Little children, it is the last time: and as ye have heard that antichrist shall come, even now are there many antichrists; whereby we know that it is the last time.* I don't want not one of you to be deceived by him, and you're probably asking yourself how we are going to recognize this antichrist character. Well, you are going to recognize him because he's going to confirm a Peace Initiative for seven years as set forth in the book of Daniel 9:27: *And he shall confirm the covenant with many for one week: and in the midst of the week, he shall cause the sacrifice and the oblation to cease, and for the overspreading of abominations he shall make it desolate, even until the consummation, and that determined shall be poured upon the desolate.* It also states in Daniel 11:21, *And in his estate shall stand up a vile person, to whom they shall not give the honor of the kingdom: but he shall come in peaceably and obtain the kingdom by flatteries.*

To reiterate, he comes in peaceably, and in Daniel 11:24, *He shall enter peaceably even upon the fattest places of the province; and he shall do that which his fathers have not done, nor his fathers' fathers; he shall scatter among them the prey, and spoil, and riches: yea, and he shall forecast his devices against the strong holds, even for a time.* Again, this scripture talks about that he will enter in peaceably. Even though the antichrist will come to you with peace, he is nothing but a master deceiver empowered by Satan himself, as set forth in Revelation 13:3–4, wherein it states: *And I saw one of his heads as it were wounded to death; and his deadly wound was healed: and all the world wondered after the beast. And they worshipped the dragon which gave power unto the beast: and they worshipped the beast, saying, who is like unto the beast? who is able to make war with him?* To all who are watching this DVD, there is still hope for you to come to Christ. Revelation 3:20 states: *Behold, I stand at the door, and knock: if any man hear my voice, and open the door, I will come in to him, and will sup with him, and he with me.* Jesus is standing at the door of your heart, knocking; all you have to do is open up and let him in. Romans 10:9 makes it plain and easy to give your life to Christ. The scripture says that *if thou shalt confess with thy mouth the Lord Jesus, and shalt believe in thine heart that God hath raised him from the dead, thou shalt be saved.* Confession is made unto Salvation. If you want to be saved, pray this prayer with me."

Everyone bows their heads, everyone except Peter; he gets up and walks out. Just as he was about to head out of the door, Cameron stops him. She steps outside with him and closes the front door. Cameron asks Peter, "Where are you going?"

Peter turns around and tells Cameron, "I'm leaving. Look, I helped you get the people together, I helped you dig up that box, but I did not agree to become some Christian. Look, Cameron, I stayed and watched the DVD, but those scriptures that Paul mentioned are so vague. I don't have time to hear all that nonsense."

As Peter is heading to his car, and Cameron is following him, he says, "You know I'm not getting on my knees to pray and sing Kumbaya."

Cameron tells Peter to wait. He then stops and turns around. "I don't get you. We both saw a lot of people vanish today, including Paul your best friend and my husband. Why won't you believe and become a Christian?"

Then Peter tells Cameron, "I will not serve a God who allows his people, whom he says he loves, to get sick and die."

Cameron asks Peter, "What are you talking about?"

Peter then explains further, saying, "I'm talking about my grandmother, Cameron, Grandma Doris. My parents left me when I was only three years old, and my grandmother adopted me. She put me through school and paid for my college tuition. After I graduated from college, my grandmother was diagnosed with stage-four cancer. I remember praying to God night and day, asking him to heal my grandmother. While I was praying night and day, my grandmother was getting worse and worse."

As Peter is talking to Cameron, tears began to fill his eyes just thinking about his grandmother.

"When my grandmother died, she was eighty-five pounds. Now what kind of God would allow his own children to go through such torture? So, at my grandmother's funeral, I said to myself that I will not serve that kind of a God."

Cameron immediately begins to embrace Peter, telling him, "I never knew that."

Peter continues talking and says, "I made Paul promise not to tell anyone about my grandmother."

Cameron speaks further to Peter and says to him, "Peter, there is something I need to tell you. The day that your grandmother died, me and Pastor McDaniel went to see her at the hospital. Pastor was just about to pray for her, but she stopped him."

Peter has a puzzled look on his face, and questions Cameron, asking her, "Why would she do that?"

Cameron tells him, "She knew that if the Pastor would've prayed for her that she would be healed of her cancer. Your grandmother said to Pastor Mc-Daniel that she wanted to see Jesus and that she was at peace with it. That night she died, your grandmother was at peace with it, and you need to be at peace as well. The Bible says in Romans 8:28, *And we know that all things work together for good to them that love God, to them who are the called according to His purpose.* Peter, I am not trying to convince you to stay, but I want you to read this scripture." As Cameron writes down a scripture on a piece of paper, she then gives it to Peter before he leaves, and she also tells him to take a Bible, which she hands him, and she tells him that he is going to need it.

Peter then gets into his car, taking the Bible and the piece of paper with him. He rolls down the window and tells Cameron that he will read it when he gets home, and then he drives off. As he drives away, one of the members of the church comes out of the house and asks Cameron, "Where is Peter going?" Cameron tells the member that Peter had to go and workout some personal issues, but he will be back.

"Come on, let's get back into the house, because I want to know everyone's thoughts on what was said by Paul on the DVD."

# At Peter's Home

Peter comes home and he sits on his couch and turns on the television. When Peter turns on the television, he sees a newscaster reporting the disappearance of millions of people across the world: some people are in distress because of their missing loved ones, rioting is going on, and looting is happening in the streets. Peter clicks the remote to go to another channel, and on that channel is another newscaster reporting the same thing. Every channel Peter turns to, there was a reporter reporting the same thing, so Peter turns off the television. He looks at a picture of his grandmother on the end table. Peter then begins to think of his grandmother and what Cameron told him about what his grandmother said to the Pastor when he visited her in the hospital on the day that she passed away.

Peter then grabs the picture of his grandmother and begins talking to the picture. "Granny, why? Why did you say that? I don't understand why you would say that?" Peter then takes out that folded piece of paper that Cameron had given him, which was in his left pants pocket. When Peter opens the folded paper, it is a title of one of the books of the Bible, with the chapter, and the verse. Peter takes the Bible from the coffee table and goes to 1 Thessalonians 4:16–17. When Peter gets there, he begins to read the verse out loud: *For the Lord himself shall descend from heaven with a shout, with the voice of the archangel, and with the trump of God and the dead in Christ shall rise first. Then we which are alive and remain shall be caught up together with them in the clouds, to meet the Lord in the air and so shall we ever be with the Lord.* Peter continues to read verse eighteen also. *Wherefore, comfort one another with these words.* After reading the scripture, Peter looks at the picture of his grandmother and says, "Therefore, you decided to die, Grandma, because of this scripture. Well, then let me go see if this thing is true." Peter goes to his garage, takes a shovel, puts it in the trunk of his car, and leaves, heading to the cemetery where his grandmother is buried.

# At the Cemetery

When Peter arrives at the cemetery, he gets his shovel out of the trunk of the car and climbs over the wall to get into the cemetery. Peter has now approached his grandmother's grave, stating to himself, "Now, let's see if the Word in the Bible is true or not." Peter takes out his shovel to dig up the coffin. Just when Peter was about to start digging, a security guard approaches and stops him by shining his flashlight at Peter. Tim, the security guard, says to Peter, "Hey, who are you, and what are you doing in the cemetery when it is closed? The sign at the entrance reads that the cemetery is open from nine a.m. to seven-thirty p.m. Monday through Saturday. It is midnight, and we are closed, sir. You are trespassing. I'm going to have to ask you to leave or I will call the police."

Then Peter tells the security guard, "I apologize for trespassing, but I need to dig up my grandmother's casket for proof."

The security guard looks at him, puzzled, and says to him, "What proof are you talking about?"

Peter tells him, "I'm talking about the proof that is in the Bible."

And again, the security guard looks at him puzzled.

"I see that you are confused, so let me explain to you that my grandmother was a Christian. The Bible says that all Christians, both dead and alive, will vanish. If that is true, then my grandmother will not be inside this casket, and the only thing that will be there is a pile of clothes. Honestly, I wouldn't expect you to understand what I'm saying."

Tim the security guard says, "I think I do, sir. See, my partner that's working with me tonight is not my usual partner; he's just filling in for my original partner, Blake, who is missing. I tried calling him, I left several messages for him, but he does not answer. Blake was a Christian as well, and if your grandmother is not in that casket, then Blake must have vanished as well. Then the things that Blake has told me about in the Bible are true. This is what I'll do. I will help you dig, because I want to see this for myself as well."

Peter tells the security guard, "Okay, but you are going to need a shovel."

Tim tells Peter, "I have a shovel back in the office. Hold on, I'll be right back." The security guard goes back to the office to get his shovel. Peter is at his grandmother's gravesite, waiting for him to return. When the security guard returns, the security guard introduces himself to Peter, and then they both started to dig. Two hours later, they reach Peter's grandmother's casket.

Then Peter begins to say: "Okay, the moment of truth has arrived, to see if the Bible is a lie or is it truth." Peter slowly lifts the casket, not knowing what he is going to see. Once Peter opens the casket, he sees that nothing is there but clothes. Peter and the security guard, Tim, both realize that the Bible is true. They both drop to their knees pray and they gave their lives to God.

Peter says, "God, I know my grandmother's in heaven with you." As Peter repents, tears start streaming down his eyes. The security guard prays along with Peter, acknowledging he was wrong and a sinner, and asking God to please forgive him for not accepting God into his heart sooner.

# Paul and Cameron's Home

At three-thirty in the morning, Peter pulls up to Cameron's house. Peter along with the security guard from the cemetery get out the car and approach the house. When Peter knocks on the door, Cameron comes to the door to open it. When she sees that it is Peter, she embraces him, and begins to say, "I knew you were going to come back once you read that scripture. It was only a matter of time."

Peter says, "That's why you gave me that scripture in the first place to read. You knew once I read it, I was going to go check it out for myself," and Peter begins to laugh and says to Cameron that she was clever, just like Paul.

Cameron says, "Well, where do you think I got it from?" Both Cameron and Peter start laughing, and then Cameron notices a man standing behind Peter. She introduces herself and extends her hand to the gentleman, and says, "May I ask what your name is?"

Tim says hello, as they both shake hands with each other. "My name is Tim McDuff. I was a security guard at the cemetery where I also helped Peter dig up the casket of his grandmother."

This news surprises Cameron! Cameron says, "I thought it was a security officer's job at a cemetery to make sure stuff like 'digging up graves' doesn't happen?

Tim says, "Yes, that is my job, but my partner Blake was one of many people that vanished."

Cameron asks Tim, "How do you know he vanished? I mean, maybe he is just on vacation. I mean, did you call, leave him a message, or even texted him?"

Tim answers Cameron and says, "I did all those things, and he didn't message me back at all. When Peter said that his grandmother was a Christian, I remember that Blake is a Christian as well. Blake would always tell me things about the Bible, but I just didn't listen. When Peter said that he's going to dig up his grandmother's grave for proof, it intrigued me, and I wanted to see if it was true, too, so I helped him."

Cameron then asks Tim, "Now that you saw the casket was empty, how do you feel?"

Tim tells Cameron, "I feel happy and sad at the same time. I'm happy that I know the truth about the Bible. I also know the whereabouts of my friend and partner. I'm sad because I didn't listen to him when he told me about Christ. If I would have listened, then I would be up there with Christ and him."

Cameron then tells Tim, "Well, at least you know now, and that you have a second chance to be with Christ. I am glad that you and Peter accepted God as your Lord and personal savior. Now, when the end comes, you will have an excellent future. Now, come on, you two, come inside, and Tim, I want to introduce you to everyone else." Then Cameron brings both Peter and Tim into the living room. Cameron introduces Tim to everyone. "Everyone, can I have your attention?" The television turns off and everyone's attention is on Cameron. "I want to introduce you all to Tim McDuff. He is a friend of Peter's and a born-again believer." Everyone says hello.

James pulls Peter to the side, and asks him, "When did this happen?"

Peter further explains to James, "When I was at my grandmother's gravesite."

James begins to ask Peter, "What in the world were you doing there?" Peter continues with his story and says, "I wanted to see if what the Bible said was true. The Bible talks about how the dead in Christ shall rise first. So, I went to my grandmother's grave, and with the help of Tim, we dug up the casket, and when I opened it, my grandmother wasn't there. That is when I realized what the Bible talked about was true."

James asks Peter, "What about what happened to your grandmother? When she was sick, you told me that you prayed day and night, yet she still died. You told me and Paul that you said in your mind at the funeral that you would never serve a God like that."

Peter recants to James and says, "I know I said that, but last night Cameron told me that on the day my grandmother passed, Pastor McDaniel visited her at the hospital. Pastor McDaniel was about to pray for her, then my grandmother stopped him from praying for her because she knew that if he would've prayed for her, she would be healed. The reason my grandmother stopped him was that she was ready to see Jesus and that she was at peace with her death. Jesus was more important to her than her own sickness. God didn't cause her to die; she wanted to die. If seeing Jesus would make her happy, who am I to stop it? When I saw there was no body in that casket, then I gave my life to God, and so did Tim."

James says, "Okay, that is very interesting, and I'm happy for the both of you," as they embrace each other.

As Peter sees everyone in the house, eyes glued to the television, he asks James a question. "What has been going on here since I've been gone?"

And James answers, "Well, everyone has been glued to the TV, because everyone in this room is trying to find out who is the antichrist"

Tim, looking confused, then walks up to Cameron and asks, "Excuse me, what is an antichrist, and what does it mean?"

Before Cameron answers him, she hands Peter the DVD and asks that he take Tim to the back so he can get caught up. Peter then does as Cameron requests and takes Tim to the backroom to watch the DVD. A church member turns on the TV because everyone wanted to look at the news, and another news anchor came on to give some more breaking news.

The news anchor begins to state, "Even though every nation is in an uproar due to these disappearances or vanishings of their loved ones, it appears chaos has taken control of the world with all the shootings, looting, and rioting going on. The governments of the world are in a panic as well because their top leaders have either vanished or have died due to airplane or car crashes. In all this chaos, there seems to be a beacon of hope. The prime minister of Pakistan, Inta Tsirhc, is the one person that has calmed everyone down. We have a video clip of Prime Minister Inta Tsirhc in his office in Pakistan making a statement to the world."

The screen turns to Prime Minister Inta Tsirhc making a national message to the world. He states, "I know that most of you in the world have lost someone due to these unfortunate circumstances and disappearances. I tell you now that this is not the time to become angry or to dispel hatred one to another. My friends, this is the time that we should come together and act as one body and one mind. We don't need to separate ourselves because of petty differences like race, types of class, and religions. Let us move forward, and together, because if we do so, we can achieve peace."

The screen switches back to the news anchor, and she continues to say, "Due to those words that were said by Prime Minister Tsirhc, calmness has come and exuberated everywhere upon the world. The governments of the world have taken control once again of their own respective nations. Chaos has been replaced with peace, and now the United Nations wants to keep this peace going, so they have called an emergency meeting. We will now go to the conference room at the UN to hear what the meeting is about."

As the screen switches, we are now shown the United Nations' conference room as we see the delegates from around the world at the table to decide the future of the citizens from around the world.

Delegate One, who represents Russia, begins with, "We have to keep this going because there is calmness around the world, but who is going to be responsible to keep this moving?"

Delegate Two representing the United Kingdom begins to speak, stating "Well, I nominate Prime Minister Inta Tsirhc to be the president of the world because he is a man of peace. I have known the prime minister for years, and all he talks about is peace. I know for a fact that Prime Minister Tsirhc will keep it going."

As soon as Delegate Two suggests Inta Tsirhc, immediately everyone at the conference agreed with the suggestion, unanimously! Delegate One turns to the prime minister and asks him, "What do you say, will you take the position of President of the World?"

Then the prime minister, with his fraudulently fake demeanor and calmness, states, "Well, if I am your last resort, then I accept this huge honor and responsibility to be President of the World."

The screen immediately switches back to the news anchor, stating, "Well, there you have it. Prime Minister Tsirhc has unanimously been elected as the President of the World. We will go back to the UN to hear the first speech address President Tsirhc will make to the world." The screen now is showing the front door of the UN, where there are cameras flashing, reporters are standing with microphones in their hands, and TV cameras are everywhere. As Inta Tsirhc begins to speak, there is a "hush" over the crowds of people as he states: "I want to thank all of you for this huge honor. Today, my main concern is that we can achieve peace, and I believe we can. That is why for my first act toward global peace as President of the World, I am instituting a Seven-Year Peace Treaty between the Arabs and the Jews. Also, to show that I mean peace, I am ordering the reconstruction on the Jews temple in Jerusalem, and this will be a sign that I have brought peace to the world, which will go down in history."

After his speech, all you can hear is massive applause from everyone as the President of the World is escorted to his car and he leaves. Inside Cameron's living room, Cameron turns off the TV, and there is nothing but dead silence, as Cameron states, "Now we know who the name of the antichrist is; none other than Inta Tsirhc, the President of the World."

One of the church members asks Cameron, "What is next now?"

After the question, everyone in the room directs their view to Cameron for an answer, as she responds, "What is next is the Tribulation."

# The Reign of the Serpent

A television set turns on, and the news anchor is telling the events that has happened four years ago. She starts off saying: "Four years ago, the world was turned upside down by the fact that half of the population of this world suddenly vanished without a trace. Worry, turmoil, and chaos had its grip on the world. During all this catastrophe, there seemed to be no hope, until a man stepped up to ease this drama that had engulfed this world, by the name of the United Nations President Inta Tsirhc. With his charismatic personality, President Inta Tsirhc has calmed the world down, and he has brought peace between the two nations: the nations of Israel and Palestine. A peace agreement has been made between Israel and Palestine. By this Peace Agreement, it showed the world that peace can be achieved."

Suddenly, the television turns off, and as suddenly as it turned off, it comes back on, and it is on the same station, but there is another news anchor person talking. This time, the news anchor person is telling the event that has happened last month.

This news anchor begins to say: "A month later, due to the United Nations President Inta Tsirhc's good faith action of peace, the United Nations has voted unanimously that the United Nations President Inta Tsirhc is to be the Supreme Chancellor of the World. We will now tune in to let you hear the speech that President Inta Tsirhc made after the United Nations voted him to be the Supreme Chancellor of the World."

As the television screen changes venues, there is a room filled with people from all over the world waiting to hear from the Chancellor of the World. In the room, you can see cameras flashing, tape recorders recording, and people holding microphones. Entering the room is Inta Tsirhc, as he now heads to the microphone to make a statement. As Inta Tsirhc comes out, he is waving, smiling, and shaking people's hands. He goes to the microphone as he begins to speak: "First, I would like to thank the United Nations for bestowing this honor upon me, of which I have greatly accepted. To tell you the truth, I didn't know that such an office like this existed. I mean, I would have never thought in my wildest dreams that I would be in this position today. People of the world, I know that we have been through great turmoil in the last month alone, and we have all lost someone special to us. I only ask that you not dwell on the negative, but dwell on the positive. I say that not to be mean, but I say that to bring you comfort. We must look at ourselves and know that we are the only ones that can help each other now.

"There are people all around the world who are looking at us now for strength and leadership. This circumstance only proves we must look only to ourselves to move forward in life. I say to you all that there is no Heaven, and there is no Hell; only us. As I look toward the future, I look at the positive. I see that this world was overpopulated. There were many people who went day by day with no food, water, or shelter. Even though we are going through this chaos, I see a hope of possibilities. A possibility that every man, woman, and child are taken care of. I am proposing a new plan. My proposal is that every country take a census of every man, woman, and child. The way the census will be structured is that every person will take a mark on their forehead or hand for the purposes of the census. With that being done, it will be an easy way for us to know how many people are being fed and clothed. Remember, you cannot buy, eat, or sell without this mark. Again, I say thank you to all of you for bestowing this great honor upon me."

When Inta Tsirhc finish speaking, the camera's venue is switched back to the news anchor's desk as she states: "That was a tape of our chancellor making his thank-you statement and his first act as the Chancellor of the World. I also want to show you all the reactions of what some of the people have said here. We have several leaders of different faiths. Listen to what each of them have to say on this subject."

The news anchor shows another tape, and in this tape, there are several different men of different walks of faith, for example, a Buddhist monk, a Catholic priest, a rabbi, and a Muslim Pastor giving their reaction to the chancellor's speech.

The Buddhist monk has on his attire with a chain around his neck, and at the end of the chain is a golden medallion, as he states: "The Messiah is an amazing man. He brought peace between two nations. I don't think anybody can do what he did, so I will do what he says and follow him anywhere."

The interviewer next goes to a rabbi. The rabbi has on his own garments and begins to say: "By bringing peace between two nations, it shows me, and it shows the world, that Inta Tsirhc is who he says he is. Now, I have heard from many people years ago that Jesus Christ was the Messiah, but now that I think about it, he was not the Messiah. Only the real Messiah can bring peace, and this Jesus that everybody spoke about to be the Messiah did not bring any type of peace to the world. All he brought was only hatred and division."

Next, the interviewer gives the microphone over to the Catholic priest who is dressed in his full attire, and he begins to say: "I agree with what these men have said about our beloved Messiah. Understand that we are all men of different faiths and beliefs. I have come to understand that all of us serve the same God. And that God is the Messiah who has come to be with us forever."

As the interviewer continues to speak to all the different religious heads, the last one the news anchor addresses is the Muslim Pastor, who is also dressed in his full attire. He begins to state, "I never thought in my lifetime that I would see peace in this world. Finally, through all the bloodshed, sweat, and tears, there is peace at last. Praise Allah, the true Messiah!" When he finishes speaking, the camera is immediately switched back to the news anchor's desk as they continue to speak about the chancellor.

"That was four years and six months ago. Even though the chancellor assured the people that every mouth on Earth was going to get fed, there are people who still won't register, and because of that, the chancellor was forced to find these people by using military force, in order to get them to take the mark, and those who didn't take the mark were going to prison, because we all feel that these people are causing division in the world. Let me add this, I believe that they are standing in the way of us reaching our highest evolution yet. The search is still on for these rebellious people, and if you know their whereabouts, you are encouraged to please call the authorities. Or you can catch them yourself and bring them to justice, it doesn't matter. Just know that you are doing your part to make this world a better place." When the news anchor person finishes, the television screen turns off.

# At the Christian Rebel Base

One year later, two men are running down a dark walkway into a warehouse full of people. Some are sleeping in sleeping bags, while others are eating tuna out of a can. The two men are carrying two duffle bags, each full of canned foods. Inside the bags are cans of tuna, green beans, potted meat, corn, Vienna sausages, sardines, and crackers. They lay the duffle bags on a table, as the people get up from their sleeping bags along with those who are reading, talking amongst each other, and sitting around listening to music on their MP3 players, to eat dinner. First, they all gather around the table to see what's for dinner. When they see what is for dinner, everybody began to grumble and mumble amongst themselves. One girl by the name of Madeline voices her opinion to everyone.

"Canned food again? Okay, honestly, I can't really take this anymore," as she looks at Cameron and tells her, "I need some real food. Like chicken, fish, steak, mashed potatoes, broccoli, cooked green beans, and maybe even a hamburger with some fries. I need other things to eat, and I'm not the only person that feels this way. As a matter of fact, if you ask anyone in this entire group, they will give you the same answer."

Then Cameron turns around and looks at everyone in the group, which consisted of forty people, and she asks them, "Everybody, do all y'all feel the same way?"

Then everyone looks at each other and say, "YES, Cameron!" Except for Peter Moore and James Wood, for they both understand the reason as to why they are eating this type of food. Cameron then asks the group "Well, why didn't anybody say anything? Why did you all just let me carry on thinking y'all liked it? Listen, I said before if you feel uncomfortable about anything, just tell me."

Madeline then says, "I was going to tell you, but we didn't want you to think that we are ungrateful for everything that you have done for us."

Cameron smiles and says, "Thank you for that, Madeline, and everyone else. I want you to know that it doesn't matter about me. I just want you to tell me how you feel. Remember, we're not just friends, we're family, and family tells each other how we are feeling."

After Cameron finishes her little speech, one of the family members, Thomas, looks at Cameron and begins to speak, saying, "I am very grateful to Jesus for touching your heart to share His Gospel with us. Even though I am grateful, I think about how my life would be if I had taken the mark. I mean, look at where we live. We live in an abandoned place, eating canned food that was found in a dumpster, and we live from day-to-day thinking it is our last."

"There are people out there"—as Thomas points toward the door—"who want to kill us, report us or, take us in because we refuse to take the mark. To be honest with you, Cameron, I can't live like this. It just seems taking the mark is so much easier."

After Thomas said his speech, all the people start to agree with him. Even though Madeline said that the reason why she didn't say anything was because she could see that Peter had gotten angry at everybody, especially at Thomas for what he had just said.

After all the murmurings, Peter is getting tired of the complaints, and begins to speak up. "Thomas, are you for real? Are the rest of you for real as well? Let's not forget how we got to this point. We were the ones who decided to live the lives that we wanted to live before the rapture. We decided to ignore Jesus, not live the way God wanted us to live, and now that He has taken his people into Heaven, we want to complain because it's hard down here. It is our own fault that we're still down here. But we still have a chance to be with Jesus.

"All of you are complaining over food and where you live. Everybody, please remember that this is nothing, and it is only temporary. Being with God is forever, eternal, and that is what we're striving for. Never forget that! Also, remember that in the book of Revelation, fourteenth chapter, verses nine through ten, it talks about whoever takes the mark of the beast will suffer the same fate as Satan, and that is eternal damnation! Now, do you want to trade that in for a piece of steak or a beachfront property that won't even last?"

After thinking about what Peter said, then Madeline, Thomas, and everyone else recants and says, "No."

Peter ends his speech by telling the people, "Keep that in mind the next time you think of saying something stupid like this."

There is a hush that comes over the room, and then James walks quietly over to Cameron and Peter and says, "Can I talk to you both in the back room for a minute?" Cameron, Peter, and James go into the back room to talk. Once they are in the backroom, James gets on Peter on how he handled everyone out there.

"Really, Peter, don't you think you were a little too rough out there with everybody?"

Peter answers him, "No, James, I don't think I was too rough because they need to know the seriousness of this all, and what will happen to them if they take the mark. I'm not going to sugarcoat it for anybody, just to make them feel good. Understand that this thing is very serious, and we must take it very seriously, because if we don't, somebody is going to lose their eternal soul, permanently."

James sees the seriousness in what Peter was saying, so he answers him back and says, "Peter, I understand where you are coming from. I just think you should tone it down just a tad."

Then Peter understood James' point of view and replies, "Okay, James, I'll tone it down just a little bit. Was that all you wanted to talk to me and Cameron about?"

"No, Peter, that was not all I wanted to talk to you and Cameron about. What I really want to talk to you and Cameron about is the fact that if you listen to how everyone is feeling, they are losing faith in God. How can we bring their faith back up?"

Cameron answers James, stating, "We can't. We can't restore nobody's faith in God, that's up to them, but what do you all suggest we do to help them out?"

Then Peter has an idea, which excites him as he shared it with his friends. "I think we can help point them in the right direction. Now, to point them in the right direction, my idea comes from Revelation 11:3."

Cameron then states, "Do you mean the two witnesses?"

"Yes, that is exactly what I mean, the two witnesses."

James is looking at the two of them, as he is looking very confused and begins to question them. "Two witnesses? What two witnesses are you talking about, Peter?"

Peter answers James, stating, "It looks like somebody's not reading the Bible enough, because in the book of Revelation, chapter eleven, it talks about the two witnesses that come from heaven. God will give them power, and they will be on the Earth to preach the Gospel of Jesus Christ for three and a half years."

And Cameron says, "Now that you mention it, I heard there were two men in Washington at the Capitol preaching the Gospel."

Then Peter says, "I think we should find a way to get everybody to Washington, DC, so they can hear them speak. By doing that, Jesus will restore their faith. What do you all think?"

James becomes uncertain and says, "I don't know, Peter. It seems a bit risky to me."

Cameron then looks at Peter and says, "I think James is right. That does sound a bit risky, but honestly"—as she looked at James—"I think it will help them. Now"—as Cameron looks at both James and Peter—"this is what I propose. We let them in on it, and we'll see what they think, and we'll take it from there. How does that sound?"

Peter said, "It sounds fine to me," and, unbelievably, James says, "Me too."

Cameron is excited and pleased with Peter and James agreeing. "Okay, great," says Cameron. "We will talk it over with everybody else at Bible study tonight after dinner." Peter and James agree with Cameron, and they leave the back room to eat dinner.

# Government Base

Next, the story takes us into a gray building, and inside the grey building are government agents dressed in black suits. There are men and women walking in the lobby. Down one hall, at the end is a door which is the only door in that hallway. Behind that door is a room filled with men and women working on computers. Inside that room, there is another small room, and inside that small room are five men sitting around a rectangular table having a meeting. The five men that are sitting around the rectangular table is the Chancellor of the World, a.k.a. Inta Tsirhc, talking with his four head agents who were demons in human form. Their names were Richard, Dean, Darren, and Drake. Inta Tsirhc speaks out about his accomplishments.

"I must say that I have accomplished a great deal in just these past few years. I have obtained peace with a peace treaty between two countries. I have won the whole world over with my kindness and my wisdom. The world has made me chancellor over everything, and now everyone on Earth is pledging their loyalty to me by receiving my mark. Now, I can finally say my will is being done."

Right then, Richard, who is one of the antichrist prophets and soldiers, asks Inta Tsirhc a question. "I have a question, my lord. How can you be so confident when there are people in this world that have not taken the mark?"

Drake quickly speaks up and answers for Inta Tsirhc and states, "He is very confident," as he fiercely stares at Richard, because he knows that if the media keeps showing the good things that Inta Tsirhc has done, the remaining people who have not taken the mark will then receive the mark because of Inta Tsirhc's accomplishments.

Darren, another prophet and soldier of the antichrist, then interjects his thoughts and says, "Besides, Richard, if they don't take the mark, they will die, so it's a win-win for us anyways," as everyone in the room laughs maniacally.

Dean then has something to say. Dean is another prophet and soldier of the antichrist, who was not laughing as he expresses his concerns to everyone. "I wouldn't laugh just yet because we have another problem to deal with. The two witnesses in Washington, what are we going to do about them? Because if they keep preaching, they will stop the progress of people taking the mark. Look, I remember when people were coming out on Facebook, Twitter, Instagram, and YouTube about the vaccines. It was because of them that many people didn't get the vaccine. I'll ask you again, lord Inta Tsirhc, what are we going to do about these two witnesses in Washington preaching that ridiculous gospel?"

Inta Tsirhc finally breaks his silence and addresses Dean. "That is a good question. My answer to that is this. What I will do will be to influence the people and the media to discredit those witnesses. That is exactly what I did with the people who spoke out against taking the vaccine. I will do it again. I will say things on the news like they are teaching the way of hate, they're trying to disunite the world, they're bringing chaos into our lives, and it is because of them that our loved ones have disappeared."

Then one of Inta Tsirhc's workers, Richard, becomes a little skeptical and says, "What if that doesn't work, my lord?"

Inta Tsirhc replies to him and says, "If it doesn't work and people still want to listen to those two witnesses, I will set up a perimeter with the assistance of the US army, twenty blocks east, twenty blocks west, twenty blocks south, and twenty blocks north. They will be ordered to shoot to kill any person they see on site without the mark. You see, Richard, your lord has everything under control, and by the end of this year, every person on this Earth will have taken the mark either on their forehead or on their hand, pledging their loyalty and allegiance to me," as he laughs maniacally.

# The Bible Study

Later that night, inside the warehouse where the Christians are hiding, they are having Bible study. They are sitting in a circle; some are sitting on chairs, some are sitting on soap boxes, and some are sitting on crates. Cameron is teaching Bible study, and as it is coming to an end, she asks the people if anyone has a scripture that they would like to share with everyone. Everyone begins looking at each other, seeing who has a scripture to share. Peter then stands up with his Bible in hand ready to share.

"Yes, Cameron, I would like to read from Revelation, 11:1-5: *"And there was given me a reed like unto a rod: and the angel stood, saying, Rise, and measure the temple of God, and the altar, and them that worship therein. But the court, which is without the temple leave out, and measure it not; for it is given unto the Gentiles: and the holy city shall they tread under foot forty and two months. And I will give power unto my two witnesses, and they shall prophesy a thousand two hundred and threescore days, clothed in sackcloth. These are the two olive trees, and the two candlesticks standing before the God of the earth. And if any man will hurt them, fire proceedeth out of their mouth, and devoureth their enemies: and if any man will hurt them, he must in this manner be killed."*

After he finishes reading his scriptures, he sits back down. Edward then states to Peter, "What do these verses talk about?"

Peter answers his question without hesitation and says, "It talks about the two witnesses that are going to come down to Earth from Heaven and preach the gospel for three and a half years. God is going to give them so much power, and if any person tries to harm them, fire will come out of their mouths to be spewed upon their assailants. They will also have power to shut up

Heaven, so that it will not rain, and they will also have power over the waters to turn it into blood."

Then Edward says to Peter, "I would like to meet them."

Cameron then chimes into the conversation and tells Edward and everyone, "Well, if you really want to meet them, you can, because they're at Washington, DC, right now as we speak, preaching the Gospel."

Then everyone in the room gasps and talks to one another about it, as Cameron continues to speak, "Here's my question to everyone: do you want to go to see them?"

Unanimously, everyone says yes. Now, the chatter begins, and everyone starts talking with excitement in their voices.

Peter then addresses the crowd and tells everyone, "Okay, everyone, calm down. I know everyone's excited, but I must let you know that it is very dangerous to get there. Are you ready to take the risks? Do you all still want to go?"

One of the Christians, Madeline, says, "I know it's dangerous, Peter, but I speak for everyone in this group when I say this. We all want to go; despite the danger, we really want to meet the two witnesses." She then turns to Cameron and asks her if she could make it happen.

Cameron tells Madeline, "Yes, I can, but I really want to let everyone here know that by doing this you're taking a risk of exposing yourself. I mean, you could get killed. Now I'm not trying to scare you into not doing this, but I want to let you know what you should expect and the possible consequences."

Then Thomas states to Cameron, "We know what we are in for, but in our eyes, it's worth it."

Then Cameron replies to Thomas with "Okay," then she looks at Peter and James, and tells them, "Let's go figure out how we are going to get everybody to Washington by next weekend."

Then all three go into the back room to strategize a plan to get everyone to Washington, DC.

# The Christians' Secret Meeting

Later that night, while everyone was asleep, Cameron goes into the back room to do a virtual secret meeting. In the meeting, it consists of forty-one people who are leaders in their respective Christian rebel groups. These are the groups of people who refuse to take the mark, and there is one group for each state. Cameron sits down in front of forty-one small projectors. After Cameron sits down in front of the projectors, she turns on the projectors, and then forty-one people appear in the room, enabling her to see the person who is representing that group. The way they can do a secret meeting without being detected by the antichrist and his minions is that they found a signal hidden in the satellite, that way they can do meetings anytime.

Cameron starts off first with the meeting by stating, "I would like to thank all of you for agreeing to meet with me at this late hour."

Julie, a leader of one of the Christian rebel groups, speaks out, because it was so late, and due to the time of the meeting, she was irritated, and says, "Cameron, it is late, so I hope you have a good reason for this late meeting."

Cameron then commences with her conversation addressing the entire group. "I have a very good reason for this late meeting, Julie. Has anyone in this meeting had to deal with people in your own respective groups who are losing faith in God because of the situations that they are in?" After Cameron poses that question, everyone starts looking at each other, nodding their heads as a sign of saying yes.

Then Ralph, a leader from another group, speaks for everyone. "I speak for everyone when I say that we all have some people like that in our own group. The issue is that each day, more people are losing faith with no remedy."

Cameron then continues again, stating that she had a remedy. Then Julie asks Cameron, "Okay, Cameron, what is your remedy?"

Cameron then continues and begins to tell the group, "Well, it wasn't me who came up with this idea; it was actually one of the people in my group that did. He suggested that we go to Washington, DC, and listen to the two witnesses. These two witnesses were prophesied about in the book of Revelation, chapter eleven. With my group talking to the two witnesses, it will show that the Bible is true, God is coming back again, and their faith will be strengthened mightily."

Julie then gets on board and tells Cameron that she thought it was a good idea. "But I have two questions to ask you: First, how is your group going to get to Washington in the first place, because you are in California, not Washington? Which brings me to my second question: How does your idea help us?"

Cameron then attempts to answer Julie's questions in the order that she has presented it to Cameron. "Well, let me answer your first question. You asked me how my group is going to get there. Well, me and my husband's friend Johnny owns his own plane. Johnny taught me and my husband how to fly, so I'm going to fly us there on his plane, which is in an abandoned airfield a couple of blocks from where we are located now. It is abandoned because after the rapture, people stopped coming to work, and plus people, including Johnny, had gotten caught up in the rapture. Johnny's plane is still there, so we are going to leave for Washington, DC, at night. The night sky will help us in not being detected or seen.

"We are going to land in another abandoned airfield which I found in Washington, DC. Then we are going to take the sewers the rest of the way to get to the steps of the Washington monument, where the two witnesses will be posted. This way, we will not be spotted by the antichrist's minions, and my group will be able to hear the two witnesses. Now, for your second question, you asked how this pertains to everyone else. Well, I have come up with an idea that when we hear the two witnesses, every group will be able to as well. The way that happens is that I'm going to hook a camera to my shirt with the speaker in it, and the same way we transmit to each other when we do our meetings is the same transmission we're going to use so everybody can see the witnesses. I'm going to give you the exact time when we're at the Washington monument, so everybody can hear the two witnesses. But it's up to everyone here to get their group together to be able to hear it on the TV screen."

Cameron begins to smile at the people with a hopeful look on her face and says to them, "That is the only way it's going to work, so what do you all think?"

Everyone looks at each other and nods their heads, one by one, and even though everyone agrees, Ralph shows his concern by speaking out and stating, "Cameron, I am going to be honest with you. It sounds very dangerous because not only are you putting your group at risk by going to Washington, but you're also putting our group at risk by using our only hidden signal that we have."

"Even though it is risky, it is also worth it, because by hearing the two witnesses, the others believers' faith in God will be restored."

Julie then thanks Cameron for being brave. As Julie opens her arms and air hugs Cameron, she tells her, "Cameron, I just want to tell you that you are very brave, so be careful out there. We are praying for you and the rest of the group for God to protect you all."

Cameron replies to Julie and everyone else, telling Julie and the group, "Thank you. Thank you to everyone. Remember, we are doing this for the kingdom of God. Also, let us pray that others who have not taken the mark will also hear, believe, and they, too, will want to be saved. I will see you all later, and thank you for meeting with me. Good night," as everyone's projectors shuts off.

# The Antichrist Secret Meeting

The meeting takes place in a boardroom. In the room is a rectangular table with five chairs, two on the sides and one at the top. Five men come in to sit down to have a meeting. Darren and Dean are each sitting in a chair on one side of the table. Richard and Drake are sitting each in a chair on the other side of the table. Inta Tsirhc is sitting at the head of the table. Inta Tsirhc starts off the meeting by stating, "Welcome. We are here to talk about the two witnesses and the fact that we don't know the location of the rebel Christians."

Darren says to Inta Tsirhc, "My lord, here's what we do know. We know that the rebel Christians are going to try to get to the two witnesses that are in Washington. What we don't know is how they are going to get there."

Inta Tsirhc then piercingly looks at Drake, Richard, and Dean and says to them, "I know you have that covered, right?"

Richard instantly says, "Right, my lord, we have it covered. We have twenty blocks marked off on all sides. If anybody tries to cross the line, the men have their orders to shoot to kill."

Richard then asks Inta Tsirhc a question, "My lord, what about the witnesses? I mean we can't touch them because they blow out fire, so what about them?"

Inta Tsirhc answers Richard and says, "No need to worry about the two witnesses. I will take care of them myself. You all just take care of those rebel Christians who will try to get near them. Those two witnesses can preach all they want to, but if nobody's there, who is going to hear them? My concern right now are the rebel Christians, for they have not taken the mark, and they're liable to convince other people not to take it either. We need to find them. It is imperative that they are found and killed."

Drake then says to Inta Tsirhc, "I understand the importance of finding the Christian rebels. I have a theory that all the Christians in the United States are somehow connected to each other. If we can find one Christian rebel base, I believe we can locate the rest of them and eradicate them. My thing is, we're trying to find out how, but I don't have the slightest idea."

It is at that point that Inta Tsirhc compliments Drake and tells him, "I like your idea, Drake," with a deviant smile on his face, but he tells Drake, "I have an idea how we can locate all the Christian rebel bases in the United States. You four do not need to concentrate on finding all the Christian rebel bases, just leave that to me. All I want you to do is concentrate on making sure no one will be able to talk to the witnesses in Washington. Before this week is over, I will have captured every Christian in the United States. If they don't take my mark, then they'll die, and that's good for me. So, either way, I win. The Bible says it is given to me to bring war on the saints and to conquer them." Then the antichrist lets out a maniacal laugh and tells everyone, "Meeting is adjourned! It is time to make history!"

# The Decision

James and Larry are carrying two bags each filled with canned foods, and they both are going down a dark alley together. The dark alley leads to a fork in the road. Both roads end up merging back together, and the road then leads to the warehouse where the Christians are living. One road is going northwest, and the other one is going southwest. The two men are deciding which road to take. Larry tells James that he thinks they should go this way, pointing towards the southwest road.

Then James says to Larry, "No, Larry, I think we should go down this road," as he is pointing towards the northwest road. "Because it doesn't have that many hills on it, and since we are carrying all this stuff, it would make it easier for us to walk."

Larry finally agrees and tells James, "You're right, but this road is the fastest way to get to the warehouse. The people are hungry, James so, we got to get to the warehouse expeditiously."

Then James comes up with an idea and says, "I tell you what, Larry, this is what we'll do. I will go down this road"—pointing towards the northwest road—"and you will go down that road"—pointing towards the southwest road. "Both roads come back together, and I will see you when we meet back up."

Larry agrees and says, "That sounds fine with me, James. I will see you later. Bye for now."

James and Larry then commence to going their separate ways, down two different roads, which will meet back up together further down the road. As James is walking on the road, he sees a man from afar off, standing there, waiting on him. As he gets closer, he sees that the man is Inta Tsirhc, and the antichrist says, "Hello, James. How have you been doing?"

James has a startled look on his face as Inta Tsirhc walks towards him. James tells Inta Tsirhc, "I know what you want, and I know who you are. You're not going to get me to take the mark, so you might as well just kill me."

The antichrist responds and says, "I'm not going to kill you, James. I just want to applaud you for what you have sacrificed over your life. But there is a question that boggles me?"

James states to him, "What is your question?"

"My question is, how can you serve a God that sat back to watch and allowed all those things to happen to you when you were a child?"

James answers, "What do you mean sat back?"

The antichrist answers James and says to him, "What I mean, are the facts about your mother and father. Wasn't your mother an evangelist at your old church, and your father was the head deacon and president of the Men's Department? Your father loved your mother, but your mother had an affair with the Assistant Pastor of that church." As the antichrist is speaking to James, he begins to show remorse and sadness on his face. The antichrist  continues to speak to try to discourage and manipulate James. "When everybody in that church found out, they talked bad about your family. It was so bad that your father left you and your mother. All because of the embarrassment he suffered because of your mother's affair that she had with the Assistant Pastor. What about the Assistant Pastor? He went and got married to another woman and became Pastor of another church congregation. What happened to your mother? She was so embarrassed that your mother became addicted to alcohol, and she died in rehab. Why would you serve a God like that? A God that would allow a child to go through all that? He literally sat back and watched your childhood be destroyed. I tell you the truth, James, I can't see how you can devote your life to a God who doesn't love you. James, I love you, and that is why I'm here tonight." The antichrist then holds out his hand and invites James to take his mark and begins to manipulate James by telling him that he will show him the love and care that he should have gotten when he was a child. Although James knew the truth of the Word of God, he was yet contemplating as to what he should do.

In the meantime, Larry is waiting on James as he is approaching the road that merges both small roads together. Larry sees James walking down the northwest road. James is yet carrying his two bags, and on his right hand Larry sees that he is wearing a black leather glove.  Larry says to James, "Man, James, it took you long enough."

James then responds back to Larry, "I guess it was longer than we thought."

Larry agrees with James and says, "I figured that. James, what is it with the right glove? Are you trying to be like Michael Jackson or something?"

James answers him and says, "I see you got jokes! But since you are being so nosey, my right hand was so cold, so I put a glove on it to keep it warm."

After that short conversation, James and Larry head towards the warehouse, where everybody is waiting on them, and very hungry. When everyone sees Larry and James walk inside, everybody runs toward them and snatches the four bags of food and begins to eat.

Cameron asks the group a question. "How does everyone feel about having Bible study while we are eating our dinner?" Some of the people are nodding their heads, signaling yes, while others are saying yes. Everybody gathers around and sat in a circle, eating dinner, and having Bible study. James didn't want to do Bible study, so he makes up an excuse to leave. James then starts in with his excuse, as he gets up from the table and everyone starts to look at him, and he states, "What!? I must keep watch to make sure that we don't have any unexpected guests." As James leaves outside to keep watch, Peter begins to look at James suspiciously as he walks out the door.

# The Plan

Cameron and Peter are in the warehouse in the backroom figuring out a plan to get to Washington, DC. Peter tells Cameron, "I say we leave from here on the bus at twelve-thirty a.m., and the bus is painted black. That way we can use the darkness for camouflage, and we should arrive at the airfield about one. Now this is where the part of my plan ends, and your part of the plan begins."

Cameron says, "Nice, Peter. That is a good plan. When we get to the airfield, everyone will board the plane. I will fly us there, and we should be in Washington at the airfield by two a.m. When we touch down in Washington, James will tell us how we will reach the two witnesses unseen."

Peter starts looking around, questioning the whereabouts of James. "Where is James anyways? I haven't seen him since he left out of the Bible study to keep watch outside."

Cameron chimes in and says, "I know, I haven't seen him either, and we need him so we can know what route that we are going to take to get to the two witnesses?"

As soon as Cameron finishes saying what she had said about the two witnesses, James comes running in through the door, and Ralph walks in after James. James then apologizes, "Sorry for being late but I had to make sure that I had everything in place so that we would be able to speak to the witnesses."

Cameron then asks James, "Okay, James, what is the plan?"

"Well, the antichrist has doubled the guards on the street, plus the two witnesses have moved from the Capitol to the Washington Monument, so we're going to have to take a different route. This is the route we're going to take," as James brings out a map of the streets of Washington that leads to the Washington Monument. "We are going to be traveling through the sewers, which leads to the Washington Monument. We will be taking the sewers from the airfield that Cameron will be landing us in. We should get to the Washington Monument undetected. That is my plan, what do you think?"

Peter tells James, "I like it," and shakes James' hand. "This will be a good way to slip past Inta Tsirhc's soldiers."

Cameron smiles at James and says, "Good work." She then turns her attention to Ralph and asks him, "Now, Ralph, do you have the device so that we can make contact with the other Christian hideouts using the satellite without Inta Tsirhc's people locating us?"

Ralph then pulls out a small black device and puts it on the tabletop on top of the map. "Yes, I will hook this device to our computer to set up a live feed when we talk with the witnesses. This device will block all security alarms, so we won't be detected when we do our live broadcasting with the witnesses."

James then states, "Those guys will not detect us when we broadcast, will they?"

Peter picks up the device and says, "I get it, this is an alarm detector," and Ralph assures him, "With this device, we will not be detected."

Cameron, then says "So, we have all sections covered for Washington, and we have this device that will allow us to broadcast to every Christian freely. We leave here at twelve-thirty a.m. to go to Washington. Okay, let's get some sleep, so we will have strength for later."

After all the plans have been made, James heads outside to the roof to look out. Ralph is heading to his sleeping bag to get some sleep before they leave later tonight. Ralph is stopped by Peter before he can get to his sleeping bag, so that he can talk to him. Peter then askes Ralph, "Can I talk to you for a minute?"

Ralph says to Peter, "Sure, Peter, what do you want to talk to me about?"

Peter answers Ralph and says, "I want to talk to you about that glove on James' right hand. Did you ever see him take it off?"

Ralph begins to think about Peter's question and then answers him, saying, "Now that I think about it, no. I have never seen him take it off or seen him without it."

Peter responds back to Ralph, "Interesting, very interesting. Okay, thank you very much, Ralph."

Ralph replies to Peter, "No problem, Peter."

Ralph then turns away to go to his sleeping area to go to sleep. But before he can lie down, Peter says to Ralph, "Let's keep this little conversation between you and me, Ralph," and Ralph agrees and replies "Okay, no problem. Goodnight, Peter."

Peter replies to Ralph, "Goodnight, Ralph."

As Peter is heading to his sleeping area to get some rest before leaving for Washington, he keeps thinking about the conversation he and Ralph just had.

# Getting There

It's twelve-thirty a.m. and the Christian rebels are dressed in black sweatshirts and sweatpants. They are all loading on the bus to get to the airfield. Once they are inside the bus, Peter drives the bus to the airfield. The bus approaches this abandoned Madison Airfield. One of the Christian rebels asks a question. Madeline says to Cameron, "Why is this airfield abandoned in the first place?"

Cameron tells her, "This airfield is abandoned because it was never used after the Rapture by anybody. My husband and I had a friend named Jason who flew his plane to deliver packages for a living. Jason also taught me and my husband how to fly, but after the rapture, this airfield became abandoned because all the pilots that flew the planes were saved. That means they were part of the massive amount of people that disappeared in the Rapture."

Then Madeline said, "Wow, that's heavy. How come you didn't accept Christ? I mean, you knew that your husband was a Christian?"

As Cameron begins to tell Madeline a little more about herself, she shares with her, stating "I got saved at the same time Paul did, but I backslid. In my backslidden condition, Paul met Jason, and Jason taught me and Paul how to fly planes. In return, Paul led Jason to Christ, but, in my opinion, Paul would of done it anyways. Jason accepted the Lord and began to do the work as a Christian, but I stayed in a back-slidden state. So, when the Rapture came, Jason was caught up to meet the Lord in the air, along with the other saved pilots. With the other pilots leaving the airfield, this place became abandoned."

Cameron continues telling her story and tells Madeline, "I am so thankful that God found us all and made a way for us to be saved, even during this dark time. Before the Rapture, my husband was saved, but I wasn't. I would go to the clubs to party, dance, and drink. My husband Paul would be at home praying for me. I mean, he knew what I was doing, yet he still prayed for me."

After Cameron told her story, then Madeline felt comfortable to tell her story, stating "I'm glad God allowed me to see the truth, because I could have gone down the same path as Jason before he accepted Christ. When my parents left, because they were Christians, I went crazy, my cousin Ralph here"— as she touches him on the shoulder—"found me, and he brought me here.

After Madeline finishes telling her testimony, Cameron continues stating, "I'm thankful God found us all and made a way for us to be saved even during this dark time." Then Madeline tells Cameron, "Well it looks like God heard your husband's prayer, because look at you now. A saved woman leading a group of Christian rebels. I know if your husband was here, he would be so proud of you!"

After Cameron heard the encouraging words from Madeline, tears begin to stream down Cameron's face, as she tells Madeline, "Thank you, Madeline, and I know that your parents would have been very proud of you, too."

After the plane landed onto the airfield, Peter gives everyone instructions on what they were going to do next. "Okay, everyone, we're here at the airfield. Let us board the plane so Cameron can take us onto Washington." The plane that everybody boarded was a commercial plane that Jason had always flown, a man that Cameron and her husband knew before the rapture. Everyone boards the plane, and Cameron flies the plane to Washington. Once the plane lands in another abandoned airfield, James leads everyone to an abandoned warehouse, and inside the warehouse, it leads to a big sewer pipe. The Christians walk through the sewer to avoid the soldiers that are standing above them on the street. As everyone is walking, Peter asks James a question, "James, this is good. We are walking right past the soldiers, right underneath their noses. How did you come across this amazing pathway to the two witnesses?"

James answers back and says, "Well, I knew somebody out here who worked at this airfield, but after the Rapture people stopped coming to work, and the place became abandoned. Now, my friend who worked at the airfield told me about this warehouse and how it has a sewer entrance on the lower level. That is how I came up with this idea of slipping past the guards."

Peter tells James, "Brilliant, James! This is just brilliant." Then Peter looks and sees another path in the sewer. When the Christians emerge from the sewers onto the streets, the streets look desolate. Nobody is on the street, so they walk forward towards the Washington monument. As they are walking towards the monument, they see two men. Each man is dressed in sackcloth clothing.

# The Two Witnesses and the Trap

When the Christian rebels saw the two witnesses, they saw two men having on light brown sackcloth clothing. They were dressed in the sackcloth clothing from head to ankle and they were wearing biblical sandals on their feet. As the Christians approached, Cameron speaks up and asks a question. "Are you the two witnesses that were spoken of in Revelation, Chapter 11?"

Witness Number One answers her and says, "Yes, we are they that were spoken of in the Bible."

Cameron continues talking to the two witnesses and says to them, "The Bible says you're to be on this Earth for three and a half years. The Bible says while on this Earth, you two are to preach the Gospel. Is that true?"

Then Witness Number Two answers her and says, "Yes, that is true, we are here to preach the Gospel."

Then Cameron asks him, "What is the Gospel?"

Witness Number Two answers her and says, "Cameron, you should know by now. I sense that there is another reason why you and everyone else are here."

Cameron then confirms his beliefs and says, "Yes, there is another reason why we are here. See, it has been over three years since the Rapture has taken place. And in every state of the United States, there are Christian rebels who live in hidden areas, but their faith has been shaken because of the situation that they live in. They see all the peace and comfort the antichrist said that he will provide if they take the mark, even though they know the outcome of what happens to them if they take the mark. But every day, Christians are giving in and taking the mark. They are giving in because of the things they have seen on the TV, and I don't know what else to do. That is why I came to you two thinking maybe you both can help us."

Witness Number One tells Cameron, "They cannot do anything but what the Lord has commanded them to do, which is to preach the Gospel. God has given us all a choice, and that choice is life or death. That is a decision that every person must decide for themselves, I can only tell you that."

When the witness says that, Cameron turns on a switch that turns on her camera, then Ralph turns on the switch which activates the satellite signal, so that every Christian rebel base in America can hear and see what the two witnesses are saying. What was unknown to them is that by Ralph turning on the switch, it also activates a homing beacon that showed the location of every Christian rebel base that was in every state in the US. Now the Antichrist knows where all the Christian hideouts are located.

# The Betrayal

Inta Tsirhc is wearing an all-black suit. He is sitting in a chair in a conference room. Then Drake walks in to tell him the information of the location of all the rebel bases. Drake starts off by saying "my Lord, the Christians are in Washington talking to the two Witnesses and they have turned on the satellite which has activated the locator. Now we have the location of all the Christian bases that are in the United States. When they turned on the switch our computers lit up like a Christmas tree." Then Inta Tsirhc said "good! Fax the addresses of every Christian rebel base to each law enforcement agency in each of the states where those bases are located and arrest them all. Once they are in prison they will have two choices, take the mark, or die.  Just like that, the Christians lose and the Antichrist wins, as Inta Tsirhc begins laughing hysterically, and stands up looking outside the window he looks up and says to God, it is not your will, but my will be done. Inta Tsirhc looks back at Drake with his eyes red and speaks with a deep demonic voice "why are you still here, go get it done." Drake apologizes repeatedly, my apologies my Lord, I will get it done, as he leaves the room.

Inta Tsirhc is looking again out of the window, and he speaks again with a deep demonic voice stating to God, "Yes, my will," and as he spoke, his eyes become red, and a snake tongue shoots out of his mouth and quickly inverts back inside his mouth, and he begins growling like a beast.

Back at Washington DC, Witness Number One tells Cameron and everyone with her, "When you choose Jesus, you are choosing life."

Witness Number Two speaks also and says, "Jesus Christ said he is the way, the truth, and the life. The end of the path to Jesus is eternal life, and the end of the path of the antichrist is death and eternal damnation. A person has a right to choose what they would want to do with the life they have."

While Witness Number Two is talking, soldiers and the police are busting in the other Christian rebel bases' doors and arresting all the Christians. Witness Number One tells everyone, "Before you leave, I leave you with this encouragement: Don't let what you see entice you to choose the wrong path. Faith in God is believing the impossible and believing the unseen. As you can see, we are the two witnesses, the two witnesses that the antichrist does not want you to hear. Why? Because we are living proof that God's love and mercy are still here, even during the tribulation period. I leave you with this question, Jesus has faith in you, but do you have faith in Jesus?"

At that point, James comes running around the corner and tells everyone, "The soldiers are coming! We got to get out of here," James says to everyone.

Then Cameron shuts off the camera switch, and Ralph shuts off the switch that connects them with the satellite. As everyone is running out, Cameron looks at the two  witnesses and says to them, "Thank you both for your encouraging words."

Then Witness Number Two replies to Cameron, "All the glory goes to God, but go, and we will slow them down."

Everyone is still running out of the building, and Witness Number Two continues to talk to Cameron, telling her, "You are doing a good job; keep this group together, but there's something you need to know, you have a betrayer in your group."

Cameron then asks Witness Number Two, "Who is it?"

He tells Cameron, "Everybody's gone, so I cannot point the person out, but I tell you this much, the person will reveal himself very soon."

Cameron ends the conversation with "Thank you."

The soldiers come around the corner, and they see Cameron, and they tell her to stop with their guns pointing at her. The two witnesses turn around toward the soldiers, open their mouths, and fire comes out of their mouths, and every soldier was burnt to ashes. Some of the Christian rebels see it, and they are astonished by it. James tells all the Christian rebels to keep running towards the sewer they came out of. All the Christian rebels are in the sewer, heading toward the entrance that led to the airfield. The last people to enter the sewer are Ralph, Cameron, and James. Ralph lifts the sewer lid to let Cameron go in first, but as soon as he opens the lid, James shoots him in the back. Ralph falls down dead. Cameron turns around and sees James with a gun in his hand. When Cameron sees James' act of betrayal, she tells James, "You! You are the betrayer!"

James tells Cameron, "That's right," as he finally takes off his glove that was covering his right hand to show his 666 mark located on the back of his right hand.

Cameron is devastated, and asks James, "How come? Why, you knew, and you still did it?"

How, blah blah blah blah," James said laughingly. "You are the one who is gullible and easily manipulated. Inta Tsirhc made me an offer that I would have been stupid to refuse."

Then Cameron told James, "Gullible? You are the one who is gullible, James. I don't know what he said to you to make you decide to go to his side, but you have made the wrong decision, a decision that was made probably in the 'heat of the moment,' forgetting about the eternal home that you would be going to when you chose the antichrist's road."

James then tells Cameron, "I believe I made the right decision because I am on the winning side. As you were talking to the witnesses, you turned on that switch that activated the satellite relay, so all the Christians around the United States were able to hear the witnesses speak. What you didn't know is that it was a trap, because as soon as you turned on that switch to connect to the satellite feed for all the other Christians to hear it, there was a locator signal setup by Inta Tsirhc himself. Every Christian rebel base was lit up like a Christmas tree, and Inta Tsirhc's soldiers were able to locate every base in the US. Now, everyone is either dead, arrested, or they took the mark."

Now, when Cameron heard this, tears begin to fall from her eyes, as James continues to spew his diabolical scheme. "Now that everyone is heading back to the airfield through the sewer, there is a band of soldiers waiting to arrest all of you at the end of the tunnel," as James laughs maniacally. "You see, Cameron, everything has been taken care of."

Cameron then decides to question James, stating, "I don't understand, James. Why did you do this? I mean, you saw the DVD, you read the Bible for yourself, so why?"

Then James askes Cameron, "Cameron, why are you so interested in the why? What you should be interested in is the now, because now is the time that you need to choose," as he held a gun to her head. "Choose to get the mark and live, or not, and then a bullet will split your skull."

Cameron then begins to speak to James under conviction, with boldness in Jesus Christ, and says, "Then I choose life with Jesus, which means I choose the bullet, because I will not take the mark."

James then tells Cameron, "Fine, Cameron, suit yourself. Just to let you know, I never liked you anyways, so this is a treat for me. Goodbye, Cameron."

And right as James is saying his so-called goodbyes to Cameron, he hears a gun click behind his head, and it is Peter, telling him, "Drop the gun, James, and back away from Cameron."

James then turns around and sees Peter standing there with a gun in his hand. Then James says to Peter, "What are you doing? We are best friends. We have been best friends since we were children!"

Peter agrees with James and tells him, "You are right, James. We are best friends, but what about Paul? We were best friends with Paul, and we were friends with him since we were children. We all befriended Cameron in our teenage years, not to mention you were the one who befriended her first. As I recall it, it was you who talked Paul into going out with Cameron, and not to mention, you were the best man at their wedding. Have you forgotten all that, James?"

James replies to Peter with, "No, I haven't."

Peter continues, "So why the sudden change, then?"

James begins to tell Peter, "The change is I now see the truth that Lord Inta Tsirhc showed me."

Peter then asks James, "What is the truth? Please, enlighten me."

James then begins to tell Peter what happened and how the antichrist, unbeknownst to him, manipulated him. "The truth is, Peter, why would I serve a God that allowed my parents to get a divorce when I was a child? I grew up having no father, and God knew that my mother was having an affair with the Assistant Pastor, but God stood there and did nothing. My dad was so embarrassed when the truth came out that my father left the church, my father left his family, so my father left me behind. My mother became a drunk and an alcoholic because she was so ashamed of herself. My mother was an Evangelist, and now she became a drunk. My father was a deacon, and now I don't know where he is. Why would I serve a God like that? A God that would allow me to go through so much pain as a child? So, once Inta Tsirhc showed me that, I began to see things a whole lot different and a whole lot clearer. The truth is, the God that Paul served, and Cameron serves, and you, doesn't love nobody but himself. I will not serve a God like that."

Then Peter gives one more attempt to try to help and encourage James by saying, "Yes, I know what happened to your family, James. Remember, I was there. But if you believe that is the truth, you are more lost than I thought. James, just like Adam, Eve, Joseph, David, the children of Israel, and Jesus Christ, your parents had the freedom to choose, just like you, but they made the wrong choice. Oh, about your father, your father was a Christian rebel who was the first to be killed by Inta Tsirhc. So, your Father made a choice not to take the mark; now he's going to be with Jesus in Heaven. Inta Tsirhc didn't tell you that part, did he?"

James is stunned at the news and upset and replies to Peter, "Well, looks like my dear old dad picked the wrong side, just like you and Cameron did."

Then James tries to point his gun at Cameron, and Peter tells him, "Excuse me, James, don't even try, so put the gun down now."

James then begins to tell Peter, "Oh, so you're going to shoot me now? Doesn't your Bible say 'thou shalt not kill,'" and Peter says, "Yes, yes it does say that, but I began thinking about that scripture. Why would God say that? I thought to myself, then I realized why. Because we are brothers in Christ, and we are not supposed to be killing each other. Now when it comes to you, it is a different story in your case. You see, you have already been marked to go to Hell, and once you get the mark, there is no coming back, so I'm sending you there by way of special delivery." Then Peter shoots James in the chest, and James dies.

Peter grabs Cameron by the arm and says to her, "Come on, Cameron. We got to get out of here!"

Then Cameron says to Peter, "How? There are soldiers waiting for James at the end of the tunnel we're trapped in."

Peter assures her, "No, we're not. I had a feeling about James, so I found another route in the sewers just in case. It does not lead to an airfield, but it leads to the forest outside of Washington, DC. Madeline is leading them. I figured we can hide there for a while."

Cameron is so happy to hear the news and tells Peter, "Good job, Peter!"

Peter tells Cameron, "Thank you, and anyways, Inta Tsirhc is not the only one who thinks around here."

Afterwards, Cameron and Peter go down to the sewer and they escape as well. They leave Ralph, who is their friend and brother, they leave James as well, who is the betrayer. They left them both dead in the alley.

# The Death of the Witnesses/Inta Tsirhc
# War on the Saints.

As Cameron and Peter make their escape, Inta Tsirhc arrives in the alley with a squad of soldiers with him. He looks for the rest of the Christians, but all he finds is Ralph and James, who are both dead. Darren comes running up to Inta Tsirhc to give him the news concerning the rebel Christians. "My lord, we just seen on the news, reports that all the Christian rebel hideouts in every state have been raided. We have captured every Christian that was in there and they're now in prison. They have two choices: choice number one, they take the mark and live; or choice number two, they don't take the mark and they will die. Now, this Christian rebel group was not at the airfield. We discovered that there was another route in the sewers, but as we were going down the path to follow them, we discovered a cave-in. We think that one of the Christian rebels set a bomb in there to cause a cave-in so that they would not be followed."

Then Inta Tsirhc tells Darren "Take some men into the sewer and dig out that tunnel so that we will be able to know where the Christians went."

Darren replies with "Yes, my lord," as he left to fulfill the command that was given to him by Inta Tsirhc.

Inta Tsirhc then walks pass the two witnesses as he is heading away, one of the witnesses says something to him. "Lucifer." As Inta Tsirhc looked back at him, "What's wrong? Don't you like to hear your real name? You know you're going to lose.

Then the second witness says, "He's right, you've read the story, you already know what it's all about, and what is about to happen next. You know the end, so why fight?"

Then Inta Tsirhc replies to the two witnesses by saying, "I know what the story is all about, and I know how I'm going to end. But these gullible and easily manipulated people don't know. By everyone taking my mark, those are souls that He"—and Lucifer points towards Heaven—"will lose to me, and that is the reason why I fight." Then Inta Tsirhc looks down at his watch, and then he looks at the two witnesses and says, "I believe it's time for you to be going bye-bye."

Inta Tsirhc then places his right hand on one of the witnesses' chests, and his left hand on the other witness's chest. When Inta Tsirhc does that, a flame in the shape of a sword comes out of both witnesses' backs, which is parallel to their hearts, and both witnesses fall to the ground dead. Inta Tsirhc un-emotionally walks away, and a soldier runs up to him and says, "My lord, we got through all the rubble to look for the Christian rebels, but as soon as we got to the end of the tunnel, the Christians were nowhere to be found."

Inta Tsirhc then becomes so upset when he hears the news, as the soldier asks him "What do you want to do?"

Inta Tsirhc instructs the soldier, "Tell every citizen of the world that if they see a Christian, make a citizen's arrest, and bring them in, and if you or any soldier sees a Christian, arrest them, and bring them in. If they refuse to take my mark, kill them, and burn every Bible you find. It is time to bring war on these saints and drag them out of hiding. It is not His will"—as he points towards Heaven—"but mine be done.

After he speaks, Inta Tsirhc does a maniacal laugh with a demonic snake-like tongue hissing out of his mouth, and Inta Tsirhc's eyes turn red as you hear the beast in him growling.

Lastly, the rebel Christians escape deep into the dark forest of Washington. There in the forest, they have a wooden table, some sleeping bags, and some food. Even though they have very little, their faith in God has been restored. Everyone is gathered around the campfire, talking, except for Peter; he goes alone in the forest walking, and he stops at a river in deep thought.

As Peter is in deep thought, Cameron comes up behind Peter to talk to him to see if he is okay. Cameron begins to ask Peter, "What are you doing out here by yourself? Is everything okay?"

Peter says, "I'm out here thinking, and yes, everything is okay."

Then Cameron says, "I'm glad that everything's okay, but what are you out here thinking about?"

Peter turns around and looks at Cameron, and with deep hurt in his heart, he says, "Tonight, I lost another best friend, so that makes two. Two of my best friends are no longer with me, and one of them I, myself, killed. I'm thinking to myself and asking what kind of person am I."

Then Cameron begins to encourage him by saying, "If you let me, I will answer that question for you. I would say to you that you are a protective and caring person. It was not that you wanted to kill your best friend, but it was just that you wanted to protect the Gospel at all costs. To tell you the truth, he wasn't your best friend anymore after he took the mark, and I believe you know that by taking the mark, James betrayed himself, you, me, and the whole group. Inta Tsirhc preyed on his most vulnerable feelings, which were his parents; so, by using his vulnerable feelings, James took the mark. Tonight, you did lose a best friend, and I'm sorry about that, Peter."

"Can I tell you one more thing?" Peter says.

"Yes, go ahead."

"You will see Paul again. You keep living a saved life, and I guarantee you that you will see Paul again," as she looks up at the sky. "Paul made the right choice in choosing Jesus Christ, and you, Peter, made the right choice by choosing Jesus, too. Never forget that," as they begin to embrace one another.

Peter tells Cameron, "I thank you from the bottom of my heart," and Cameron tells Peter, "Thank you, too, for showing me the right way to Christ Jesus."

Peter tells Cameron, "No problem, what are best friends for!"

Looking surprised, Cameron states, "What! We are best friends?"

Peter assures her that she is so right. "You are like a big sister to me, so let us join the others, sis."

As they walk back to the camp where the other Christians are, Madeline approaches Cameron with a question. "Cameron"—as Madeline counts on her fingers—"okay, let us get this together. Ralph is dead, the other Christians are arrested, and James betrayed us all. Did I miss anything?"

Cameron tells her, "No, you didn't miss a thing."

Then Madeline asks Cameron, "What are we going to do now?"

Larry interrupts and says, "Well, we can listen to the news on the radio," as Larry pulls out a radio out of his bag and turns it on to the news station. That way we can at least hear what is going on out there."

As everyone listens to the news, the radio announcer begins to speak, stating, "This is interesting and very, very encouraging. The Chancellor of the World, Inta Tsirhc, asks that all the citizens of the world turn in every Christian they find and if they see any Bibles, burn them. Now people all over the world are turning on Christians, right and left, and burning Bibles in the streets. It is amazing to see the unity of people, because you have people of all nations, creeds, and races coming together for one common goal, and that is to turn in all Christians that are hiding."

Cameron then turns the radio off; she looks at everyone as she sees fear in their eyes. Cameron then addresses the people.

Cameron is scared as well, and she speaks, "Everybody, I understand that you are all scared, and to tell you the truth, I am too. But one thing is for certain, we cannot lose hope. Hope that this is not going to last long. Hope that there is a better future for us, and the hope that eternal life is waiting for us. We must put our trust in God, and I promise you God will see us through all of this. Madeline, you asked me a couple of questions minutes ago, what are we going to do now? I will now tell you what we are going to do. We are going to wait and wait for the second coming of Jesus Christ!"

After killing the two witnesses in Washington, D.C., Inta Tsirhc has made war with the Christian rebels, by ordering his people to report those who have not been marked, those who are caught praying to God, and report those who are reading a Bible secretly in their homes. Cars are now arriving at abandoned buildings, and agents, soldiers, and officers are jumping out of their cars and going into the buildings with the intent of arresting as many Christians that they can find. They are busting down doors with their boots, and believers in Christ Jesus are being dragged out of abandoned buildings by the police and thrown into the back of black vans. The believers are being taken to prison with an angry mob waiting for them outside the prison walls as they arrive. The mob is shouting and throwing stones, bottles, and trash at them as they enter the prison.

The crowd outside the prison walls was shouting saying beat them rebels, (while some of the crowd members were threatening the rebels by holding a noose in their hands). Shoot them rebels, behead them rebels, and burn them rebels. All the while they were throwing things at the entrance of the building and all around it. There was a barricade and guards all around the building. The guards were making sure that the hostile crowd that was outside the prison couldn't get in and also making sure that the prisoners couldn't get out.

# The Meeting

There are four men who are dressed in black suits and sitting in a conference room of a government building: Richard, Drake, Darren, and Dean. They are sitting and waiting for Inta Tsirhc, (the antichrist), to come in to start the meeting. Inta Tsirhc then comes in, dressed in a dark blue suit, brown shirt, brown tie, and dark shoes. When Inta Tsirhc comes in, everyone gets up from their seats as a sign of respect.

Inta Tsirhc goes to his seat, sits down, and then he tells everyone, "You may all be seated," as everyone sits back in their seats. The antichrist starts off by saying, "Let's get this meeting started. We will hear first from Richard, Drake, Darren, and then Dean. Okay, Richard, report on how things are going with the citizens of the world. I know that everybody was shaken up when they saw the two witnesses a month ago rising from the dead in the streets and ascending into the clouds."

Richard responds by saying, "Yes, everyone was shaken up by the ascension of the witnesses into the clouds; but everyone still remains loyal to you. The media has made everyone think that the two witnesses that ascended into the clouds were a hoax. The rebel Christians were just like the soldiers in the Bible, who lied to the people telling them that the disciples stole the body of Jesus out of the tomb."

The antichrist says, "Good, we need to keep everyone on our side and not theirs. Okay, Drake, your turn to report. How are the police doing in finding and arresting all the Christians?"

Drake begins his report, "The police are finding Christians daily, and the jails are filling up fast throughout the world. I told the wardens in charge of each prison to start torturing and killing some of Christians. The death of a few Christians will serve as an example to the rest of the world that we are not playing games. They have only one choice and that is to take the mark or suffer the consequences. Isn't that right, Darren?"

Darren looks at Drake and says, "Yes, you are right, Drake. My lord, Inta Tsirhc, me and Drake are working together on this," as he is pointing to Drake. "Drake is making sure that the Christians are all thrown in jail, and I am forcing them to take the mark. if they refuse, Drake told the wardens of each prison to torture them. If they still refuse, death will become their best friend."

Darren's report pleases Inta Tsirhc, as he begins to laugh with a maniacal sound, and then he states, "I like that. Excellent, very excellent! I like the fact how you"—as he looks at Darren—"and Drake are working together. I want to make sure that the message is loud and clear to these rebel Christians that we are not playing with them! These Christians are going to learn that either they take my mark, or they will die! Which now, is your turn Dean. I need your report. Update me on those Christians who were in Washington that heard those two witnesses. Have they been found?"

Dean is afraid of the report he is about to give Inta Tsirhc, for he knows Inta Tsirhc will not like it. "No, my lord, they have not been found."

Intra Tsirhc then becomes very angry with Dean and asks him repeatedly, "What do you mean NO! It has been a month since the two witnesses were killed when the Christians escaped my trap."

Then Dean responds to the antichrist, "I'm sorry, my lord, but ever since they escaped our clutches, it has been hard to find them. It is like they have some type of barrier that cloaks them from sight."

Intra Tsirhc rises slowly from his chair, looks at Dean, and with a deep demonic voice, he says to Dean, "I don't care what type of cloak you think they have; you LOOK HARDER, BECAUSE I WANT THEM FOUND! Do you hear me?"

As Dean fearfully responds to the antichrist, "Yes, my lord."

The antichrist begins to walk towards the window, as he speaks and addresses everyone in the room, stating, "Ninety-five percent of the world has taken my mark, which means that they are on my side. The five percent who do not have my mark, are a problem to me; as you know it's those Christians that managed to escape my clutches. I want them all FOUND!"

Inta Tsirhc stops from looking out of the window and turns around to look at everyone else in the room and says, "Let all the Christians know around the world that if they don't take my mark, they will be instantly tortured then killed." Inta Tsirhc then looks back out of the window towards the sky in continuing with his speech, and he states, "He is returning soon, and that means a war is coming," as Inta Tsirhc continues to look out of the window. "We need to be on one accord, just like at the Tower of Babel. When Jesus returns, he will see his own creation ready to fight against Him. That is a victory within itself! So, Dean, finding those rebel Christians is now your top priority."

Dean replies to Inta Tsirhc, "Yes, my lord. We shall double our efforts to find them."

The antichrist then says to the remaining people in the meeting, "Good. Now, for the rest of you, continue to do what you are doing and make sure that you stay on top of things."

Everyone responds to the antichrist in one voice, "YES, MY LORD."

Inta Tsirhc then ends by saying, "Okay, this meeting is adjourned." The antichrist walks out of the room, and then everybody else leaves.

# The Forest

In Washington, DC, deep in the forest are four people, two men and two women. Their names are Johnny, Megan, Kenneth, and Aniyah. They are walking through the forest, and they are lost. Their frustrations are rising, as they don't know where they are going. Megan stops in her tracks and says to Johnny, "We have been walking in this forest for what seems like forever. You don't even know where you are going anyway."

Kenneth agrees with Megan as he stops walking and says, "Yeah, she's right, Johnny. All this walking we are doing, I don't believe you know where you are going."

All the discussions have prompted Aniyah to stop as well, as she turns to Johnny and says, "John, I concur. You are leading us, and how can you lead us when you don't even know where you are going?"

Johnny then turns around to look at them and says, "All of you are right. I don't know where I am going, but what I do know is that those Christians who were there in Washington, DC, when the two witnesses were speaking to them were last reported in this area before Inta Tsirhc's goons raided our base in Oregon. There are reports that have said that the Christians had escaped into the forest that night. This exact forest. So, I believe that they are here. We must find them, and we will. Come on, let's keep moving. We need to find them before the sun goes down."

As the group continues to walk deeper into the forest, the evening time comes upon them. They soon approach a clearing, and there is a man sitting on a rock. The man is wearing a black T-shirt, blue jeans, black tennis shoes, and a black baseball cap. There is a vision of a man from a distance that is sitting on the rock, and when they came closer upon him, it was Peter, and he stuck out his gun at them and begins asking them questions.

Peter says to them, "Hold it right there!" And all four of them stopped and put their hands in the air. "I don't see any mark on your foreheads. Let me see your hands. I want to see if you all have been marked."

Johnny says to Peter, with his hands yet posted in the air, "No, we have not been marked. We are looking for the Christians that were seen in Washington, DC, when the two witnesses were there. Have you seen them around here? Because we heard that they came this way escaping the antichrist's soldiers."

Peter responds to them by saying, "I've seen them, but why are you"—as Peter is walking towards them—"looking for them?"

Then Cameron comes out from a bush that is behind Peter, and states, "Okay," as she puts her hand on Peter's arm where he held the gun on them, and she lowers the gun. "Peter, stop giving them the third degree. But I do agree with Peter's question. What are your names, and why are you all looking for the Christians?"

The first person to speak is Johnny, who introduces himself, and pointing to Megan says, "This is Megan, Kenneth, and Aniyah. Me and Megan were with the Christian group in the state of Oregon. We were watching and listening when the Christians had the conversation with the two witnesses. Then, suddenly, the antichrist soldiers came in and arrested all of us. Everyone was arrested and thrown in the truck to be taken away. Not everyone got caught. Me and Megan had gotten away, so we decided to go and look for the Christians. The last message we had heard from or about the Christians was that they are still in Washington, DC, hiding in the forest. Me and Megan were hoping that we could wait for the return of Jesus Christ with them. As we were looking for them, we found Kenneth and Aniyah looking for a place to hide from the antichrist. Both are Christians, and they, too, are awaiting the return of Jesus Christ. We all want to wait with them. Is it okay?"

Cameron responds, "Well, you found us. Come, follow me to the place where we are hiding." They all follow Cameron into the bushes, and as they pass by Peter, he looks at them suspiciously, so he walks behind all of them.

As Johnny is walking besides Cameron, he begins to ask her, "Peter doesn't like us that much, does he?"

Cameron answers and says, "Don't mind Peter. Ever since his best friend James betrayed us, which led to the raid on all the rebel Christian bases, Peter has been very cautious and suspicious of anyone that comes near us."

"Okay, I perfectly understand that, Cameron. So, what happened to James?"

Cameron says, "Well, it turns out that James took the mark but hid it from us, so that he can fool us. When he betrayed everyone, he tried to get me to take the mark. When I said no, he pulled out a gun to kill me. Then Peter took out his gun and shot him, James died. Peter killed his best friend, and he has never been the same since. Now he lives with the guilt of killing someone even though they had the mark on them already." Johnny sorrowfully responded as he felt bad for Peter saying "wow! That is heavy. I can see why he is like the way he is. I understand, thank you." Cameron then said to Johnny, "that is very heavy, and I'm glad that you understand. They all approached a huge mountain and next to it was a river, okay everyone, we are here." Megan said to Cameron, "here????? As she is looking around, I don't see no hideout?"

Peter says to Megan, "Of course you don't see anything, that is why it is called a hideout. We are hiding in plain sight, and the entrance to the hideout is under water." Then as he spoke, Cameron and Peter jump into the river first, and then everyone else does it as well. Underwater, you can see that there is a hole that serves as an entrance into the mountain. Johnny, Megan, Kenneth, and Aniyah follow Cameron through the hole that is in the mountain.

Cameron turns around and says to her four guests, "Welcome to the Grace Base, where salvation abides, and we are eagerly awaiting the coming of our Savior." Cameron then continues to give the four guests a tour of the cave.

Back where the Christian rebels are hiding, there are three levels. The first level is the main level, where the people meet for Bible study, prayer, eating, and meetings. On the second level is where everyone sleeps, and each person has their own sleeping bag. The third level has these holes in the mountain; the holes were the size of a man's hand. These holes are used to keep watch for enemies, that way they will not be ambushed. On the third level, Peter is sitting in a chair, keeping watch.

Then Johnny overtly says to Cameron, "Wait a minute, I've got a question. Where did these Christians come from? Because I thought all the Christians were arrested and taken to prison."

Cameron then stops the tour and turns around towards Johnny and begins to say, "There were many Christians who escaped the antichrist soldiers. When they did, they all came here for refuge and to wait for the return of Jesus Christ. I had a feeling that is why you all came here, for we are all brothers and sisters in Christ. Who am I not to help my fellow brother and sister in Christ?"

# The Prison

In a maximum prison in Washington, each cell has twenty Christians in it, and there are Christians who fear what is about to happen to them next. Other Christians in the cells have a determined look on their faces, showing that they are not going to take the mark. An officer walks out of a back room into the area where the jail cells are located, and when the head guard walks into a cell, he sees a man encouraging Christians to stay strong. When the people in the cell see the head guard, they immediately get quiet as the head guard says to everyone listening, "I am going to make this easy for all of you. To avoid any kind of torture, I am offering you a one-chance and only one-chance offer to escape a beat down. All you must do is just renounce Jesus Christ and take the mark, and after that, you can leave here free."

Suddenly, the prisoner that was encouraging everyone in the cell begins to speak out on behalf of all the prisoners to the head prison guard, stating, "We will not renounce Jesus Christ, nor will we take the mark!"

After the head guard hears what the encouraging prisoner had to say, he becomes extremely upset and looks at the prisoner who spoke out, then he looks at everyone else in the cells and says, "Okay, if that is the way you all want to play it, then fine by me." Then, immediately, three extra prison guards rush into the cell where the one prison guard is, as the head prison guard continues to tell the prisoners, "To tell you the truth, I am glad you all refused to take the mark, because I really prefer to do it this way, anyway. All right, men, do it!"

Then the guards take the prisoner who spoke out and handcuff both wrist to one cell bar, with his back turned towards the other prisoners. Another prison guard walks into the cell with a whip in one hand and a bucket of water in the other hand. The other prison guards that are holding the prisoner begin to tear his shirt off, leaving his back bare for all to see. Then the head prison guard begins to speak, stating, "Now, let's see, since you choose not to renounce Jesus Christ nor take the mark of the beast, you will get beat, and the number of lashes you will receive on your back will be equivalent to the amount of people you influenced that are in this cell now, times two. That means forty-eight lashes on your back. Okay, guards, we're ready to begin."

The prison guards that came in with the whip inside the bucket of water to strike the back of the prisoner with the whip. As the guard is striking Prisoner Number One on his back, bruises are forming on his back, and blood is streaming out like a river. As the guard is whipping Prisoner Number One, his face shows the unbearable anguish and pain that he is experiencing. The other prisoners see the punishment that Prisoner Number One is receiving, and the prisoners are all screaming and crying for him.

After the tenth lash, the head guard looks at the rest of the prisoners and speaks to all of them. "Hold on for a minute, guard." Then the guard stops hitting the prisoner with the whip. "You know all this can end right now. All you must do is renounce Jesus Christ and take the mark."

As soon as the head prison guard says that, another prisoner speaks up with a question. "Are you sure, or are you just lying to us?"

The head prison guard then answers him with a smile on his face, stating, "I assure you the guard will stop; you have my word."

Then the looks and faces of all the other prisoners in the room change, and you can tell that they are thinking about it as they begin to look at each other. Suddenly, the prisoner that was receiving the beatings musters up some strength and begins to speak to all the prisoners in the cell, telling them, "Listen, I know that I am in pain, but it is worth it. Remember, this is for Jesus, and I am more than satisfied to drink from the cup that Jesus drank. No matter what happens to me, don't give in and don't give up." When he finishes talking, he turns his head, awaiting further punishment from the guard.

The rest of the prisoners that are in the cell say unanimously all together, and with a determined voice, "We will not renounce Jesus Christ, nor will we take the mark!"

The answer that the prisoners gave angered the head prison guard even more, as he turns back toward the guard who was whipping Prisoner Number

One and says, "Fine, you can continue with the beating." As the guard continues to beat the prisoner with the whip, the prisoner is screaming in agony with every strike. Then he begins to look up toward the heavens; he cries with a loud voice, "Even through the pain, I give you praise and glory. Thank you, Jesus, for saving me."

As the prison guard continues to hit him on his back with the whip, the prisoner cries out, "Thank you, Jesus," after every hit, without fail. When the guard is finished beating the prisoner, the other guards uncuff the prison bars, and the prisoner falls on the ground, lifeless and soaked in his own blood. The head guard then looks at the other prisoners in the cell and points his finger to another prisoner.

The head prison guard then said to the prisoners, "We will be back in thirty minutes, and if you all do not renounce Christ and take the mark of the beast, you, my dear girl, will be next to receive a beating. Believe me, I will not take it easy on you because of your sex or age, little girl." The head prison guard, along with the rest of the guards, leaves the prison cell and the prisoners alone with the bloodied prisoner. Then all the prisoners came over to comfort their friend.

# Grace Base

Johnny and Kenneth approach Peter to talk to him. Johnny starts off by saying, "Hi, Peter," "Can me and Kenneth talk to you for a minute? We have a question that we want to ask you."

Peter looks at them and answers, "Sure." Both gentlemen pull up a chair and sit down next to Peter. "So, what do the both of you want to ask me?"

Kenneth says to Peter "Well, it is mainly me who wants to ask you the question, and Johnny just came along with me for support. I was curious about how you gave up everything to end up here?"

Peter, looking puzzled at Kenneth's question, then states, "What do you mean by that statement, Kenneth?"

Kenneth begins to further explain himself and says to Peter, "Well, I heard some information about you, Peter. You were a very successful tax attorney, and your business was constantly growing, as you were a wealthy man. I mean, you were living in a loft, and your lifestyle was extravagant. The women you dated were A-list beautiful. I just don't get how you could just give all that up just to follow Jesus. I see it like this: You gave up everything to follow Jesus. Now you live in a cave full of spiders, bugs, worms, and all types of creepy things. Not to mention, the food that you eat does not compare to the food you were eating back then. The food you eat now looks like table scraps; I mean, you were eating filet mignon, and now you're eating bologna. Bottom line, Peter, what convinced you that this life is better than your old life?"

Peter chuckles, and then he answers Kenneth. "That is a very good question. To tell you the truth, if the shoe was on the other foot, I would be asking you the very same question, so let me answer it for you. My father and mother abandoned me when I was a child. I lived with my grandmother, who is my father's mother. My mother's parents died, and my grandmother's husband left her for another woman when my father was a boy. Since I was a child, my grandmother adopted me. My grandmother raised me from a child on up to an adult. I graduated and went to college, but what I did not know is that while I was in college, my grandmother developed stage-four cancer. When I graduated from college, I went back home, and I found out my grandmother was sick. Now, my grandmother was a devout Christian, so I prayed to God every day to heal my grandmother. Do you know what happened to her each day I prayed? She got sicker, sicker, and sicker until the day that she died, and when she died, that is when I decided that God doesn't live in my heart. I thought to myself, 'What kind of a God will sit back and allow his child to go through days of pain?' Instead of healing my grandmother, God took her life. I said to myself, 'That is not a God I would want to serve.'

"I began to start depending on myself and nobody else. I became a successful tax attorney, and life was going good for me. Now, Cameron's husband, Paul, was a devoted Christian and one of my best friends. I was there when he was raptured up, but I still didn't believe in God. His wife, Cameron, told me that my grandmother's Pastor came to visit her in the hospital, and she confessed to my Pastor that she was ready to go. My grandmother told her Pastor that everything down here was taken care of and there was no need for her to stay. My grandmother wanted to die, and then Cameron gave me a scripture to read in 1 Thessalonians 4:16—17. It talks about how the dead in Christ shall rise first, and after I read that scripture, I immediately jumped into my car and headed for the cemetery to dig up the casket of my grandmother. When I dug up her casket, looked inside to find only her clothes, wedding ring, and the Bible I placed there. I then realized that God is real, and my grandmother is with Him. On that very night, I gave my life to God and chose to follow him anywhere. As I kept reading the Word on my own, I discovered that all the things that you see like the mountains, trees, water, women, cars, houses, and money, they are all temporary, where God is eternal. I would rather stay by God's side and live with him for eternity than to go to Hell and die. I made a conscious decision that Hell is not going to be my destination. Being with Jesus in Heaven is going to be my destination. It is because of Jesus, Kenneth, is why I gave up everything to follow him. I hope I was able to answer your question."

Kenneth and Johnny are blown away by Peter's answer, then Kenneth says to Peter, "You did, and thank you, Peter, for answering my question."

Peter then looks at Kenneth and Johnny and says to Kenneth, "No problem, Kenneth. Now I have a question for both of you. I told you the reason why I chose to follow Jesus, and I told you about my conviction. My question for both of you is, what are your convictions for following Jesus Christ?"

Johnny answers first. "Well, for me, it was my cousin Mark. Mark was saved, and he loved God. Mark always told me that God is coming back, and I'd better get saved. I would always say that he's crazy because people have been saying that for years. He then starts saying to me that, one day, he's going to disappear, and half of the world is going to disappear, along with all the babies in every hospital. Then I will know that the God that he serves is real, but it will be too late for me to do anything about it at that present time.

"When that fateful day came, Mark and I were playing basketball at the park, and then, suddenly, he disappeared. I was so surprised! Then I remembered what Mark had said about him disappearing. I went home, turned on the television and the news reporter said that all the babies in the hospitals had disappeared, along with half of the population of this world. I knew then that God was real, and that is my conviction." After Johnny finishes his conviction, it is Kenneth's turn.

Kenneth began with, "Well, I have no convictions like you two. To tell you the truth, I would like to have one for myself as well, because I am so confused. On one hand you have this man that is doing all this good in the world, doing all these great things to help mankind, but under all that goodness is actually the devil that is trying to trick us. That is why I am confused, because I don't know what to believe."

Then Peter hands Kenneth a Bible and says to Kenneth, "Here, Kenneth, take this Bible and read the whole book of Revelations. I promise you that everything that has been talked about dealing with the end times is being manifested today, and then you will know for yourself that God is real."

Kenneth takes the book from Peter and tells him, "Thank you, Peter." Kenneth and Johnny are now walking away from Peter, and while they are walking away, Kenneth is reading the Bible.

In the cave on the first level, everyone is in groups having individual Bible study. One of the Christians approaches Cameron to ask her a question. Cameron is sitting on a chair at a table, listening to the radio. This young Christian lady sees Cameron minding her own business, sitting, and listening to the radio. She asks Cameron a question. "Cameron, what are you listening to?"

Cameron replies to her, "Well, I am listening to the radio to see what is going on in the world. Since we don't have a television set, this is our only access."

The young lady asks Cameron another question. "Why are you doing this, if you don't mind me asking?"

Cameron's response to the young lady is "by doing this, I will know how close we are to Jesus Christ's return." Cameron turns off the radio to speak loudly to everyone that is in the cave. "Everyone, gather around," as everyone goes over to the table where Cameron is sitting. "I want us all to hear what is going on in the world." Cameron then turns on the radio to the news station. Cameron turns up the volume on the radio, so everyone in the cave can hear it.

The radio broadcaster began her segment by saying, "Hello, everyone. I am Veronica Michelle on the FM news station bringing you the top news of the world. The world is at a standstill with a slew of different occurrences happening back to back. On Monday of last week, every person on this earth was hit with sores all over their bodies. No one knew where the sores came from. People just woke up from their beds this past Monday morning, and there the sores were all over their bodies, covering each person from head to toe. Then on this past Tuesday, all the seas became bloodied, and all types of sea creatures began floating dead in the water. On Wednesday, blood that was in the seas went to the rivers, and the environmental sciences couldn't figure out what was going on with the rivers. Many animals, like salmon and trout, were found floating dead. The heat this past Thursday hit an all-time high of one hundred fifty degrees, and many people died from heat strokes across the whole world. On Friday, the whole earth was covered in darkness. At twelve noon, it looked as if it was eight at night.

"In every country, it is reported that a million car accidents occurred, one hundred thousand people ended up in the hospital fatally injured, and the other hundred thousand were reported dead. On Saturday, the most peculiar thing happened. The Euphrates River dried up completely. There is no blood in sight, or any sea creatures. Then, on Sunday, all over the world, there were reports of earthquakes. Many people were fatally injured, and some have lost their lives. If people weren't injured from the earthquake, they were injured from the great hell that fell from the heavens. Because of all the occurrences that have happened, the nations of the world have begun to fight amongst each other. During this time, the chancellor of the world says."

"Citizens of the world, we should not be fighting amongst one another. We must come together on one accord and stand. I am a man of peace. I abhor violence, but I will tell you the truth…. There's someone who is coming to break that peace, and will bring violence, war, and death to this world. That man is Jesus Christ. This Jesus is not the Jesus from the Bible, because I am He. I am the Messiah, and this Jesus has been jealous of me for many years. Now, he has come to destroy this world, but if we stand together and fight, not only will we win, but we will annihilate those who stand with this Jesus. Citizens of the world, stand with me and fight. Once we win this war, everything will be as it should be, and that is a unified world, because when we are unified, there is nothing we cannot do."

After the chancellor's speech, the radio broadcaster continues her report by stating, "After hearing the speech of the chancellor and the so-called messiah, every country in the world has decided to stand behind the chancellor to fight this bully named Jesus. It is amazing how unified this world has become. There are people from all walks of life from different countries, different races, different religions, and different backgrounds. They have all come together as one people, to fight in this war." Many people have unanimously named this battle, "The War of Armageddon."

After listening to the disturbing news segment, Cameron turns off the radio and addresses the Christians, saying, "Now you all see where we are. We are very close to the return of Jesus Christ."

Cameron is then addressed by one Christian with his hand raised to ask her a question. Cameron acknowledges him as he asks her, "Do you know what day that he will show up?"

Cameron answers and says, "I don't know. I cannot answer that, but what I do know is that by reading the Word of God and listening to the radio, I know that he is coming very soon, and we must get ready for him." Everyone then goes into their sleeping bags to go to sleep.

# Betrayal at the Base

Later that night, while everyone is asleep in their sleeping bags, Kenneth and Aniyah are up in a corner talking amongst themselves. Aniyah says, "Good job, Kenneth. Good job on keeping Peter busy. While you were keeping Peter busy, I was able to contact Dean and let him know where all the Christians are. I couldn't do that with Peter constantly watching me, so, again, thank you, Kenneth. We are so out of here. Very soon we will take the mark, and once we take the mark—"as she speaks, she takes his hand, and he grabs her hand, and she looks into his eyes—"our lives will be much better, I guarantee you."

Then Kenneth takes his hand back and says, "I don't think so, Aniyah."

Aniyah looks at him, confused, and asks, "Why did you say that?"

Kenneth responds by looking at her and says, "I say that because everything that is written in the book of Revelation, chapter sixteen"—and he opens the Bible and turns to the chapter and shows it to Aniyah—"has come to past."

Aniyah is still looking confused and has a shocked look on her face, and she asks him another question. "Like what, Kenneth?"

Kenneth answers Aniyah and says, "Like sores, seas turning into blood, rivers turning into blood, frequent and massive earthquakes, darkness, the Euphrates River freakishly drying up, and don't get me started with the scorching heat waves. All of it has been prophesied in the Bible. The Bible is real! Everything in it is real! Here, read it for yourself," and then he hands Aniyah the Bible.

Aniyah then becomes very angry at Kenneth and throws the Bible on the ground and tells him, "I'm not reading that nonsense! What has happened to you, Kenneth? I thought we had a plan, which was to locate the Christians and report it back to Dean. Somewhere along the way you lost sight of our goal, so, tell me, what happened to you, Kenneth?"

Kenneth looks at Aniyah and answers her, saying, "Jesus is what happened to me. I asked Peter what made him decide to leave the life of riches, sleeping in a nice bed, just to live in a cave full of bugs and roaches. Peter told me about his grandmother, and that she was a saved woman who raised him from a child on up, and how she died. When the rapture happened, that night, Peter went to her grave, and when he opened it, he saw nothing but clothes inside the casket. That scene led Peter to giving his life to Christ, and that was Peter's conviction to becoming a born-again Christian. Peter then asked me what my conviction was, and I didn't have one. Then Peter gave me the Bible and told me to read it, and in there I would find my own conviction. When I read Revelation, sixteenth chapter, I noticed that all the prophecies that are in that chapter have all come to pass."

Aniyah then looks at Kenneth in irritation, and with a sarcastic look on her face says, "Oh, really? I see Peter's life got to you."

Kenneth looks at Aniyah and says, "Yes, it did. Because after I started reading the Word of God, God started opening my eyes on a lot of things."

Aniyah is yet in a sarcastic mood and asks Kenneth "What things?"

"Well, for starters, I started to look at Inta Tsirhc's name. If you flip his name backwards, it is pronounced antichrist. The devil has been telling us who he is all along; we just did not really look at what was being said. For example, look at the word Santa. If you take the middle letter out, which is an 'n,' and put it at the end of the word, it is pronounced Satan. Look at the word Clause, if you take out u, s, e and replace it with w, s, it becomes claws, so Satan claws. You can also look up the word 'Old Saint Nick' in Google and find out that it means 'devil.' Even though the devil can change himself into an angel of light, he is still that old serpent that Adam and Eve met in the Garden of Eden. He is still that old serpent, a dragon with claws, ready to grab you because he is 'like' a roaring lion seeking whom he can devour. Basically, me, you, and the whole world have been deceived by the master deceiver, prince of darkness, prince of the air, God of this world, SATAN!"

Aniyah then becomes livid with Kenneth! And she sternly says, "That is enough, Kenneth! What you are doing is just reaching for something that is not there. The things that you are saying are nothing more than a fantasy, and you need to get a grip and walk yourself out of that fantasy world and start living. This right here is reality," as she points at their surroundings. "The soldiers are on their way here, and you are going to have to decide between them—"pointing at the Christians—"or me"—pointing at herself. Soon after Aniyah and Kenneth finish speaking, the soldiers come in from the entrance river and from the hole in the cave which they made with a grenade. The soldiers grab each Christian and put them in handcuffs to be taken to the prison.

When all the Christians are subdued in handcuffs, a truck with a drill comes in next and drills a hole in the mountain next to the river entrance of the cave. Through the rubble and the smoke, a figure walks in through that drilled entrance. The person who comes into the room is Dean, who is one of Inta Tsirhc's head men, as he walks over to the Christians. He begins to look around in amazement and says, "Wow, this is an excellent place to hide. I can see why finding you all was so difficult for me. That is why I recruited these two people right here," and then Dean puts his hands on the shoulders of Kenneth and Aniyah. "I couldn't have done it without them."

Then Cameron turns around and looks at Kenneth and Aniyah and says to them, "You two? I don't understand why you two would do this. Both of you knew the Word of God."

Aniyah then looks at Cameron and says to her with a sarcastic smile on her face, "Why do we do this? Let me help you with that answer. We were promised a better life. You see, you think a better life is with you all. Why would you think that I want to live with you people who live with bugs and ants? I would rather live in a place where I will have a mansion, a nice car, and be well taken care of. Doing this, we"—as she points at herself and Kenneth—"not only will get the mark but all those other things that I just said."

Then Peter sadly says to Aniyah, "Oh, Aniyah, you are going to have a rude awakening, but Kenneth, I have a question for you. Have you found your conviction?"

Then Aniyah butts in and says, "You know, Peter, that is a very good question that Dean and I would love to hear. Tell us, Kenneth, have you found your conviction, and if you did, what is it?"

While Dean, Aniyah, and Peter look at Kenneth, Kenneth then answers Aniyah and says, "I have found my conviction, and my conviction is this: I believe the Bible to be the holy word of God. I believe that the word of God is true, and in front of all you, I ask the Lord for forgiveness of my sins, and I invite the Lord to come into my heart, because I believe in you, Jesus."

Immediately, Dean's face turns to the epitome of evil as he spews out of his anger and says, "Fine! You have made your choice. Soldiers, arrest Kenneth as well!" Dean gets up into Kenneth's face and tells him, "I expected more from you!"

Then Aniyah walks over to Kenneth with great disappointment on her face, telling him, "You made a BIG mistake in choosing this Jesus over me!"

Kenneth reassures her and says, "Yes, Aniyah, I did choose Jesus over you. Jesus is and shall remain first in my life."

From disappointment to anger and from anger to resentment, Aniyah displays to Kenneth and tells him, "Oh, really? Since you put Jesus over me, I erase you from my life and you can go meet your Jesus today." Aniyah then takes a side arm from one of the soldiers and shoots Kenneth in the chest.

As Kenneth lies lifelessly on the ground on his back after being shot by Aniyah, he looks at Aniyah and says to her in a weak voice, "I forgive you, for you don't even know what you are doing." Afterwards, Kenneth looks towards Heaven and has a dialogue with God and says, "Lord, please forgive me of my sins and receive me into your kingdom," as he took his last breath.

Dean then looks over the body of Kenneth and says sarcastically, "Oh, how touching.Well, that's it! Soldiers, take all of these Christians to prison!" Soon after, Dean, Aniyah, and the soldiers leave the cave, and Kenneth on the ground, dead.

# The Maximum-Security Prison

In the maximum-security prison in Washington, DC, inside the prison there are forty-two cells, three levels in it, and on each level, there are fourteen cells. When the rebel Christians came into the prison, the rebel Christians saw the other Christians who were already in cells, bloody, with scars on their backs; black and bloodied eyes; purple, red, and black bruises; and with cuts all over their bodies. Each rebel Christian was thrown into a cell with only a few Christians inside each cell. Cameron looks at one of the bruised prisoners and asks, "Are you one of the band of Christians who was in Washington, DC, that was captured by the soldiers a couple of months ago?"

The prisoner says to her "Yes, each cell that you see represents a state in the United States. Some of the cells have more prisoners in them than the other cells because the soldiers tortured and killed them for not taking the mark, and they have disposed of them out of the cells. We are all the Christians who are left in these cells within the United States.

"I guess you wondering why we are still alive, and it is because they have not gotten around to us yet for questioning. You see, here, you have two chances to refuse the mark of the beast. If you refuse to take the mark the first time they ask you, you will be horrendously tortured, and on the second time you refuse to take the mark, you will then be killed."

At that moment, two soldiers enter the cell, pointing a gun at Cameron and Peter. As they grab them by the arms, one of the soldiers says to them, "Cameron and Peter, come with us. The Messiah is here, and he wants to see you two." The soldiers bring Cameron and Peter into an office, where the Messiah awaits them.

When Peter and Cameron see Inta Tsihc, he looks at them with a smirk on his face and says, "Cameron and Peter, let me say that I am so excited to meet you two people, you guys actually thought you could hide from me, but—"

As Peter cuts him off, he says, "Before you go any further, I know what you are going to say, and I know Cameron will agree with me when I say this: We will not take your mark. We know who you are," and when Peter says this, Inta Tsirhc starts getting mad. "And your plan is not going to work. Let us not waste each other's time. Kill us now and get it over with."

Inta Tsirhc then slowly turns around, angry, with his eyes as red as fire, and he says to Peter, "First, Peter, you are not wasting my time, and secondly, it is going to work. You see, Peter, you and Cameron don't realize this, but a whole lot of Christians look up to both of you. Now, if they see you two killed, they will be so afraid to the point that they will follow me instead of following him," as the antichrist points up at God.

Peter then says to Inta Tsirhc, "Once again, you are wrong. You can kill me and Cameron, and it doesn't matter. They will still follow God and not you."

Inta Tsirhc then gets so angry to a boiling point of rage, and then Peter digs in more to the antichrist and says, "I see that you're getting upset because of what I said. You should be upset, because your time is almost up, and you know full well, as I, that Jesus's return is coming very soon. My advice for you is for you to do what you need to do now, because time is almost up for you, sooner than you think."

Then Inta Tsirhc says to Peter, "I see that you have some fight in you, and no matter, it's to no avail." The soldiers then grab Peter, each of them by one of Peter's arms, and the antichrist tells him, "There is someone that you know who has been waiting to see you again; he'll beat some sense into you." The antichrist then flicks his hand, and the soldiers take Peter out of the room. The soldiers are taking Peter into another room, with his hand bound in handcuffs. The soldiers throw him on the ground and leave the room. When Peter looks up from the floor, he sees James.

Peter looks in deep shock and says, "James, you're a…"

James says to Peter, "Alive, surprised to see me?"

Peter, still looking in shock, says, "Yes, I am, but I thought you were d—?"

James finishes Peter's sentence, "Dead, that is right. See, after you, my so-called best friend, shot me in the back, I thought I was dead, too, but Inta Tsirhc revived me, and now that I am alive, I have pledged my life of devoted service to Inta Tsirhc. Now, out of respect for our past friendship, I will offer you one more time to take the mark."

Peter says "No, but no thanks."

So, after hearing Peter's answer, James looks at him with a twisted smirk and says, "I had a feeling you would say that, and that is why I asked. Now that I have asked and you refused, I can kill you without any repercussions. Oh, yeah, how I love payback." James then takes a gun and shoots Peter in the head.

As James is going back into the room where Inta Tsirhc and Cameron are, Cameron shows signs that she has been beaten up in the face, and she is still in handcuffs. Cameron looks up at Inta Tsirhc and says, "Enjoying yourself, Inta Tsirhc? You might as well kill me, because you know good and well that I will not take your mark."

Then Inta Tsirhc bends down and looks Cameron eye-to-eye and says, "I already knew that. I want you here for two reasons. The first reason is coming in right now."

In walks James into the office, carrying a dead Peter on his shoulder as he drops Peter on the floor. Cameron immediately starts crying when she sees Peter dead on the floor, and when she looks up, she is surprised to see James alive. She says to him, "James, you're a—"

As James finishes Cameron's sentence by saying "Alive, yes, I know. I already went through this with Peter," as James looks down at a dead Peter on the floor. "I don't want to deal with you, so here is the explanation as to why I am alive. After I was shot in the back by Peter, the Messiah soldiers took me back to a lab, and the doctors there revived me. Now, I have pledged my allegiance, my loyalty, and my services to the Messiah."

Cameron looks at James with disappointment in her eyes and says, "Oh, James, you have made a huge mistake. You will find out later, I guarantee you."

Inta Tsirhc then chimes in after Cameron finishes her sentence and says, "Well, what a nice reunion this is. Three friends back together again. With a little twist, you, Cameron, are still alive, while Peter is lying here—"as the antichrist's right hand is pointing towards the Peter—"dead, and James is here with me, alive. The second reason is that you are going to be a sacrificial lamb for the world to see. Once you die, I will gather them to battle Jesus when he returns." Inta Tsirhc then looks at James and says, "Take her." Then the antichrist looks at the soldiers and instructs them to take the dead body out of his sight, as Inta Tsirhc says, "I have to prepare for my speech."

# The Gathering

While on top of Mount Nabi Yunis in Palestine, Inta Tsirhc, along with the captains of the world, each captain is representing their own country, and each captain's army is at the bottom of the mountain. Cameras are also on top of the mountain to record the speech, so that the people all around the world can see and hear the speech that the Messiah is about to give. The camera is on Inta Tsirhc, as he gives his speech to the world. Inta Tsirhc then looks at the captains and the cameras and begins to speak.

"Citizens of the world, we stand on the brink of unity and prosperity. There are only two people standing in our way. One of them is her," as Inta Tsirch infers as the soldiers, along with James, bring a bloodied Cameron, who is bruised and battered, almost to the point of unrecognizable. Cameron has been brought up the mountain and thrown down at the feet of the antichrist like a piece of meat by the soldiers. As the Messiah continues, "This lady right here"—the cameras zoom in on her face—"is Cameron White. She is the leader of the Christian resistance. All the Christians will have been eradicated off the Earth because she is the only Christian that is alive, and right here on this mountain, she will be executed today. To show you that, by her death, we are moving closer to peace and prosperity." Inta Tsirhc then turns to the soldiers and says to them, "Get the chopping block and put her on it." The chopping block has been brought up the mountain by more soldiers, and they place Cameron on the chopping block to be executed for the world to see.

As the antichrist continues with his speech, he states, "By pulling this lever down, it will be the end of Christianity and the beginning of peace and prosperity." Then Inta Tsirhc pulls the lever down and kills Cameron, as her head falls to the ground. Everyone on the top of the mountain, and at the bottom of the mountain, and all around the world are celebrating the death of Cameron White. The antichrist continues by saying, "Now with Cameron out of the way, there is only one man that stands between us and our peace and prosperity, and the name of that man is Jesus Christ. So, let's get ready for war!

Everyone on top of the mountain and at the bottom of the mountain raises their right hand in giving a battle cry! Right after the armies of the world make their battle cry, instantly the sky cracks open, and all you can see is a man sitting on a white horse. The man who sat on the white horse: his face was so bright that all you could see was an image, his eyes were like flames of fire, and on his head are crowns, and he has a name written on his forehead that nobody knows but him. He wasn't alone, because behind him are the armies of Heaven, which consist of the saints and all the angels of Heaven. The armies of Heaven attack the armies of the earth, and the armies of Heaven prevail against the armies of the earth. The man who sat on the white horse is called faithful, true, and righteousness, who rode down to the top of the mountain where the generals were. When Inta Tsirch saw that the battle was lost, he flees the mountain before the man on the White Horse can get to him, and he escapes to Jerusalem to hide in the palace. Back at the mountain, when the generals try to look at Jesus, he is so bright that they cannot look at him.

Jesus was surrounded by generals, and their guns are drawn, facing him. When Jesus turns and just looks at half of the generals, they fall down, dead, and the rest of the generals immediately fall on ground dead. Inta Tsirhc is hiding in the palace and consulting with four of the head demons, Dean, Drake, Darren, and Richard.

Inta Tsirhc begins to speak to his head demons, "Okay, Jesus has returned to Earth, and you all know that we can't stop him."

Right after the antichrist barely spewed the words out of his mouth, two of God's angels come into the room, and Angel Number One says to Darren and Richard, "Okay, Darren and Richard, it's time to go."

Angel Number Two then looks and says to Drake and Dean, "You guys are not forgotten; it's time for you to go too." Richard, Drake, Darren, and

Dean start to run. The angels of God stretch out their arms towards them, and chains come out of their hands. Those chains bound those four men, who were demons, and the angels drag the demons out to be judged.

# The Judgment

All walks of life are standing in front of this big, white throne. The being that is sitting on the throne is so bright that you can't see the person. All you can see are the image and his eyes, which are red as of fire. All the host of the angels flying left and right across the great white throne. Then four angels brought Inta Tsirhc in front of the throne. The antichrist begins to speak to God, saying, "I know, you don't have to tell me. Lake of fire here I come, but at least I will not be alone," as he is looking back at everyone who took the mark and sticking his tongue out at them like a snake. "See you all at the lake of fire."

God then tells his angels, "Get Satan out of my presence, along with his beasts and prophets. Immediately toss them all in the lake of fire!" As God speaks, instantly, a portal opens, showing a lake, but instead of water, it consisted of fire, and everybody saw the antichrist, his demons, and fallen angels being tossed into the lake of fire. Then, as instantaneously as the portal opened, it closes in like manner, for now.

At this point, James is standing next to Paul, when he heard what the antichrist said to everyone who took the mark, and James says to Paul, "Paul, what is Inta Tsirhc talking about, 'see you at the lake?'"

"Well, James, everyone who has taken the mark of the beast on their right hand or forehead will not be allowed to enter the Kingdom of God." Then James looks at his right hand and sees the mark, and he becomes nervous and replies to Paul, "No, it can't be true. I am a good person."

Then Angel Number Three, who was flying in the air, comes down and speaks to James and says, "Is that so, James? Let's look at the memory screen to see." As Angel Number Three and James look at the screen, the screen shows James taking the mark, showing James betraying the Christians, and shooting

Ralph in the back, and shooting Peter in the head. After Angel Number Three shows James of the things he had done on Earth, the Angel then turns to James and says, "From the memory screen, we see that your past actions were not good at all."

Then Aniyah looks at the back of her hand, looking at the mark and trying to hide it from God, Jesus, and the angels. Then Angel Number Four flies down and starts talking to Aniyah and says, "Why are you hiding your mark now from everyone? You were so mouthy and proud of your mark earlier, and so eager to get it, weren't you? Let's look at the memory screen and see for ourselves about your past actions." The memory screen shows Aniyah and Kenneth making a deal with Dean, who was one of the demons. They agreed upon infiltrating the Christian group to get the mark.

Then Aniyah turns around, looking at Kenneth, saying, "Ha, I'm not the only one in the memory screen making a deal to infiltrate the Christians; it was Kenneth too," as Aniyah points to Kenneth and says, "He should be going where I am going."

Angel Number Four says to Aniyah who was looking at Kenneth, "I can see your claim, but it is invalid. Do you remember when Kenneth found his conviction? He chose God over himself and most of all over you. Let us not forget that he gave his life to Christ after you shot him." As Angel Number Four is telling Aniyah about Kenneth, it is being shown all on the screen. "This is not about Kenneth but about you, so let us keep watching the memory screen." As Angel Number Four looks toward the memory screen, the memory screen shows Aniyah not only taking the mark, but she was living it up in a mansion. Then the screen cuts off, and Jesus speaks to the Angels.

Then Jesus says, "Angels, separate the marked People from the unmarked people." Then the angels begin to do what Jesus said to do, and the angels put the unmarked people on the right and the marked people on the left.

God says to those who was marked, "I sentence all of you to the lake of fire!" (Revelation 14:9–10)

Instantaneously, a portal opens to the lake of fire, and everybody on the right side and on the left side sees an abyss (the abyss is called Hell). You can hear screams coming from that abyss. The abyss turns upside down, and the abyss is sinking in the lake of fire as well. When the abyss is turned upside down, you can see people who were already in hell falling out of that abyss and into the lake of fire. As they are falling out of the abyss into the lake of fire, they are all shouting out, "God, forgive me, I am sorry. Give me one more chance," but God was not listening.

A condemned man  on the left speaks out and says… "God, I thought that you were a God of love. People are calling out to you asking for forgiveness, and yet you won't hear them. I do not see the love coming from you, so, tell me, why is that?"

Angel Number Five then flies down to speak. The angel turns to the throne where God is sitting and says, "My Lord, may I speak?"

God answers Angel Number Five, "Yes, you may."

Angel Number Five begins to speak to the condemned man. "Excuse me, sir. God is love. God has shown his love many times to you. God has sent his Son to die for your sins. God has allowed you numerous times to get it right, and he did that because he loves you. Many people have always asked if God is love, why does he allow these things to happen? What people don't understand is God gives everyone the freedom to choose, so the reason why this is happening is because people chose to do the things they wanted to do, instead of obeying God. Now, the question comes down to this: Do you love God?"

The condemned man who asked the question replies to Angel Number Five, stating, "I do love God. I did everything in the name of Jesus. When I preached, it was in Jesus's name. When I prophesied, it was in Jesus's name. When I visited the sick, it was in the name of Jesus, and when I laid hands on God's people who were sick, they were healed in the name of Jesus. If it wasn't for me," as he is pointing at a man that is in the group that is on the right side, "that man would not have known Christ."

Then Angel Number Five replies to the condemned man asking the question and tells him, "Yes, you are right. This man went to one of your tent meetings and accepted the Lord into his heart. The difference between you and him is that he meant it with all his heart, and you, on the other hand, only did it with your lips."

The condemned man replies to Angel Number Five and says, "Excuse me, my life was all about giving praise to God. Everything I did was for Jesus, for the kingdom of God."

Angel Number Five looks at the condemned man and says, "Correction, at first it was for the kingdom, but when the money started rolling in, you began doing it for your own gain. Do you remember when people were asking you to come speak at their tent services, but because they didn't have the right amount of money that you desired, you turned them down? At those ten revival engagements you turned down, a lot of people could have been saved, but because of your selfish greed, they were lost. Yes, you praised God, honored God, but it was with your lips, and not with your heart. Remember, the Lord knows the intention of each man and woman's heart, and no one, and I mean no one is exempt from this."

The condemned man looks at Angel Number Five and says, "Wait, wait, wait a minute, wait just one minute," with fear and trembling in his voice. "How can you say that when you knew I was going through financial trouble?"

Then, again, Angel Number Five replies to the condemned man, stating, "I can say that because throughout your entire life, I was assigned by God to keep watch over you and to give an account to God on how you were doing. What I have discovered is this: Yes, you've been through financial trouble, but you didn't trust God. Little did you know, God had a plan to get you out of that trouble, but you didn't wait on him, nor did you trust him; you did what you wanted to do. Now, if you will look on your right hand"—the condemned man looks on the back of his right hand—"the mark of the beast is on you, and with the mark of the beast, that means you will suffer the same fate as Satan."

God then gives further instruction to the angels, saying, "That is enough talking. Go back to your post." God then speaks to the people on the left, stating, "All of you have made your choice; you have all chosen Satan over me, so this day, I say to you, depart from me!"

As soon as God says that, the same portal appears, which leads to the lake of fire. As the people on the left are going into the portal where the lake of fire is, the people on the right start to cry for their loved ones. Some of the people on the right are crying out, saying things like "Why didn't you listen to me? Why did you backslide after I told you you can come back to Jesus? Why did you listen to your friends who believed in other religions? Why did you allow yourself to be tricked by those false prophets? Why did you allow yourself to be tricked by those false preachers? Why did you allow yourself to be under the leadership of those false Pastors, and why did you take the mark of the beast?"

Then Jesus comes down from the right hand of the Father and stretches forth his hand towards the people and says in a soft voice, "Peace." After Jesus speaks, a glow which came from Jesus went onto the people, and their tears fade away. As the people on the left are going to the lake of fire, the people on the right turn towards Jesus. All the people on the left are sucked into the portal, screaming and crying. Then they are gone forever.

# The New Earth

As God rains down fire from heaven, the whole world is destroyed. Nothing is left, but darkness has once again covered the earth, just like in Genesis 1:1. Out of that darkness, God said let there be a new Heaven and a new earth. On the earth, everything is like new. The mountains are new, the lands are new, the seas are new, the lakes are new, the rivers are new, the grass and the trees are new. After God created the new earth, the new Heaven that God created comes down from the sky and rests on a mountain. God says to the Christians to come and see, I have made everything new and I invite all my children to come and live on this earth. Now the people came out of the new Heaven to see the new earth that God has created and God says to his people, "I want you to enjoy the goodness of what I have done on this new earth."

The heaven is so bright that there was no need for the sun for light. On the top of the mountains where Heaven stood, people came down the mountain to enjoy the goodness of the Lord and to behold his glory on the earth. The last ones to come out of heaven are Paul, Peter, Cameron, and Kenneth. They come out and stand on top of the mountain to view the goodness of the Lord.

Paul says to Cameron, "Well, Cameron and Peter, with the help of the Lord, we are here! We made it!"

Cameron replies, "It took a sacrifice, but in the end, I thank the Lord we made it." Peter then walks over to Kenneth, putting his hand on Kenneth's shoulder, and speaks to him, saying, "Thanks be to the Lord, who causes us to triumph, how do you feel, man?"

Kenneth turns around to say to Peter, "I thank God for giving me my conviction. I thank God for saving me, and I thank God for giving me a second chance. I know that if it had not been for the Lord on my side, I would not be here looking at God's amazing glory. I am amazed at his works!"

Paul then speaks to everyone who could hear him. "From hearing everyone's deep gratitude and approval, I believe we all agree when I say God has been good to us," and everyone agrees and says, "Yes he has!"

Then Paul continues to speak, "Now let us all go down from this mountain and enjoy the goodness of the Lord." As Paul, Peter, Cameron, and Kenneth all walk down from the mountaintop to partake and enjoy what God had prepared for them, they begin to praise the Lord aloud with great joy for His love and His goodness towards them forever!

# THE END